Barringto

School Spelling
ictionary

hristine Maxwell and Julia Rowlandson

rrington Stoke

This edition published in Great Britain by Barrington Stoke Ltd,
18 Walker Street, Edinburgh, EH3 7LP

www.barringtonstoke.co.uk

Previously published by Barrington Stoke in 2006 as Primary Spelling Dictionary

ISBN 978-1-84299-520-4

Cover design by Latte Goldstein

Trademarks
Words in this dictionary which we believe to be trademarks have been acknowledged as such. The presence or absence of such acknowledgements should not be regarded as affecting the legal status of any trademark or proprietary name.

Typeset by GreenGate Publishing Services, Tonbridge TN9 2RN
Printed in Great Britain by The Charlesworth Group, 2007

Acknowledgements

I would like to thank the following people:

Christine Maxwell for having the original insight into creating a dictionary that can be easily used by poor spellers.

All the children who contributed misspellings which often in their opinion were how the words should be spelt!

My late father, David Driver, who tirelessly checked head words with me.

Ruth Paris for her patient editorial work and sense of humour.

Kate MacPhee and Joanna Craddock for their proof-reading skills.

Julia Rowlandson BA Hons, PGCE, Dip RSA, SpLD

Preface

To the Teacher

After the publication of the revised and updated *Dictionary of Perfect Spelling*, Barrington Stoke has had numerous requests for a school version.

In my work as Head of English in a school for boys with specific learning difficulties, I continually witnessed the frustrations of children trying to use a conventional dictionary to help with their spelling. More often or not they gave up and spelt the word phonically. In the *School Spelling Dictionary*, following Christine Maxwell's inspirational idea, they can do just this.

But when they check their phonic spelling, if they find the word in red, it is wrong and beside it they will find the correct spelling in black.

For example: eny any

They can then locate the correct spelling and check any derivatives.

For example: any ~body ~how ~one
any ~thing ~way ~where

The tilde(~) tells the user to just add on the ending to the root word.

Irregular plurals are given.

For example: wolf wolves

Verb endings are given in full.

For example: fly [flies flying flew flown]

Comparative adjectives are spelt out.

For example: funny funnier funniest

If they have difficulty finding a word, there are hints as to where else to look.

For example: Under **ci** you will find

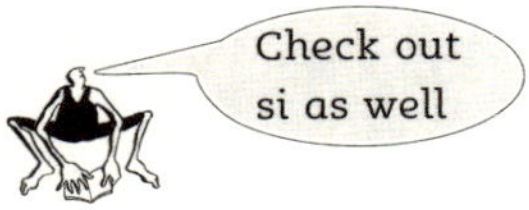

I have included some useful spelling rules which need to be taught and learnt. I found Gill Cotterell's Phonic Reference cards published by LDA an excellent resource.

To the Speller!

The English language is very hard for the person who hates spelling because groups of letters can make more than one sound. Even spell checkers find it hard! However, 86% of words do stick to rules and the tips on pages v to vii are there to help you. We call the other 14% of words 'irregular' because they do not follow rules or patterns and you need to find ways to remember them.
Pages viii to x will give you some ideas of ways to learn them.

We all need to spell words the same way to make sure that we can write what we want to say and so everyone who reads it can understand exactly what we mean.

Some Useful English Spelling Rules –
It does help to learn them!!

1. Remember vowels (a e i o u) can make a short sound or a long sound (like their name).
   For example ā as in ape [long – its name], ă as in apple [short – its sound].
   'y' sometimes acts as a vowel as well, e.g. 'cry' and 'rhythm'.
2. Have fun with words! Learn to build words from the root word, use **prefixes** (bits you add on the front) and **suffixes** (bits you add on the end).
   For example: stand, <u>under</u>stand, understand<u>**ing**</u>, <u>mis</u>*under*stand**ing**
3. 'q' always has 'u' with it and is written 'qu' like in 'quiz' and 'question'.
4. No word ends in 'v' except 'spiv' (a flashy man). Often 'e' comes after 'v' to prop it up like in 'active' and 'native'.

5. No word ends in 'j'.
6. Never write a 'k' before a 't'. Always write 'ct' as in 'fact' and 'direct'.
7. No English word ends in 'i'.
   Watch out for rule breakers: taxi (short for taxicab) and ski, spaghetti and macaroni (but they aren't English!).
8. The 'ee' sound at the end of a word is mostly spelt 'y'.
   Watch out for rule breakers: coffee and committee!
9. Double 'l' 'f' and 's' after a single vowel in a short word, e.g. spell, boss, stiff, puff. Watch out for rule breakers: us, bus, gas, if, of, this, yes, plus, nil, pal!
10. Add 's' to make a regular plural as in 'cat - cats'.
11. Add 'es' to make a plural if the word has a hissing ending like: 's - buses, x - foxes, sh - brushes, ch - churches, ss – fusses.
12. If a word ends in one 'f', change it to 'v' and add 'es' to make the plural.
    For example: leaf → leav → leaves, wolf → wolv → wolves.

    Watch out for rule breakers: dwarfs, chiefs, roofs!
13. For most words that end in 'o', add 'es' to make the plural. For example: potato + es = potatoes.

    Watch out for rule breakers: pianos, solos, Eskimos!
14. The prefix 'all' at the start of a word is only spelt with one 'l' – almost, altogther, also, already.
15. The suffixes 'full and till' at the end of the word only have one 'l' – helpful, until.
16. Remember the suffix to make an adverb is 'ly' NOT 'ley'!
17. Drop the final 'e' from the root word before adding a suffix that starts with a vowel. For example: ~~move~~ + ed = moved, like + ing = liking, drive + er = driver, muddle + ed = muddled.

18. If a word ends in a consonant + y, change the 'y' to 'i' before adding any ending except 'ing'. For example:
marry + es = marries, funny + ly = funnily.
BUT fly – ing = flying, carry - ing = carrying.
19. 'ck', 'dge', 'tch' are used after a short vowel (one that says its sound). For example: back, hedge, match.
Watch out for rule breakers: rich, much, such, which!
20. If a words ends in a single vowel and a single consonant always double the final consonant before adding a suffix that starts with a vowel.
For example: stop + ed = stopped, fat + er = fatter, hot + est = hottest, rob + ing = robbing.
21. 'ce', 'ci', 'cy' makes the /s/ sound.
For example: centre, circle, cycle.
22. 'ge', 'gi', 'gy' makes the /j/ sound.
For example: gentle, giant, gym.
Watch out for rule breakers: get, begin, girl, give, gear, geese, gift, girth!
23. 'i' comes before 'e' except after c, but not when it sounds like /ā/ as in 'neighbour' and 'weigh'.
Watch out for rule breakers: neither, foreign, seized, sovereign, forfeit!

Ways to Learn Spellings

Hear it See it Say it Do it

To remember a spelling you must –

1. Think about the word that you are trying to learn and make sure you understand what it means.
2. Divide it into syllables (chunks). You can find where they are by putting your hand under your chin and counting how many times your chin goes down when you say the word.
   For example: Sat/ur/day = 3 syllables. Note that each syllable must have a vowel. It can sometimes be 'y'.
3. Talk about which parts of the word are hard to spell and highlight them.
4. Practise spelling the word at odd times, e.g. on the way to school, in the shower/bath, etc.
5. Learn other words with the same pattern and then they will be easier to remember. For example:
   few, crew, grew, flew, blew, etc.
6. Use the learning style you like best.

If you are an auditory person: – say it aloud to yourself, sing it, turn it into a rap, quiz a friend.

If you are a visual person practise writing it; use different colours, look at the tall letters and short letters, draw pictures as clues, pretend your eyes are a camera and take a photo of it. Can you see a little word inside it?

If you are a person who likes to learn by doing things, make huge letters in the air, walk up and down chanting it, do an action which links to the word, decide how many sounds are in the word and with the palm of your hand facing you, touch a finger as you say each sound.

7. For irregular words, think of associations/mnemonics to trigger your memory. Remember, the more ridiculous your rhyme, the easier it is to remember how to spell the word.
8. Talk about it and teach it to a friend or to a parent.

Let's learn to spell the word '*people*' using a technique with a very long name – 'Neuro-linguistic Programming' or NLP for short.

1. Ask your teacher to write *people* on a card in large lower case letters
2. Talk about the bit which make it hard to learn – You can't hear the o and you have to remember the */pul/* sound at the end is spelt '*ple*'
3. Now look up to the left and visualise (imagine you can see) the first letter *p* in the air or on a wall (you can choose a colour for it)
4. Now say *p* aloud
5. Now visualise the next letter *e* beside it
6. Start at the beginning and say the two letters aloud *pe*
7. Now say them backwards *ep*

   We do this to make sure you are visualising *pe*. You will find it hard to say it backwards if you are not visualising the letters
8. Then add the next letter, that silent one *o*. Pretend you are climbing through the circle it makes

9. Now say them from the beginning *peo* and backwards *oep*
10. Now add another *p*. Make sure it is the same size and colour as the first one
11. What do you have in the air now? Say *peop* and then backwards *poep*
12. Now add a tall *l*
13. What do you have? *peopl* *lpoep*
14. Now for the last letter. Add another *e* in the same colour as the first *e*
15. What do you have? *people*. Backwards *elpoep*
16. Brilliant! Write it down
17. Now write a short sentence using it
18. Test yourself later in the day. If you think you have forgotten how to spell the word, look up to the left to help recall it. Then write another short sentence using the word.
19. Practise it every day for a week and keep your own spelling bank!

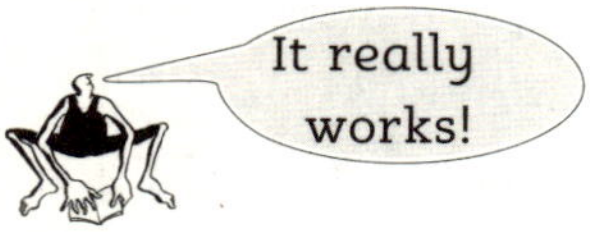

abacus
abandon
[abandoning abandoned]
abawt about
abbey
abcent absent
abdamen abdomen
abdomen
abee abbey
abel able
ability abilities
able
abnormal abnormally
abolish [abolishing abolished]
Aboriginal Aborigine
about
above
abowt about
abracadabra
abrawd abroad
abroad
absail abseil
absant absent
absawb absorb
abseil [abseiling abseiled]
absence
absent absent-minded
abserd absurd
absorb [absorbing absorbed]
absorbent
absurd absurdly
abuse [abusing abused]
abuv above
abyus abuse
accelerate
[accelerating accelerated]
accelerator acceleration
accent
accept *[take] except *[but]
[accepting accepted]
acceptance
accident
accidental accidentally
accommodation
account [accounting accounted]
accountant
accross across
accur occur
accurate accurately
accuse [accusing accused]
ace
acelerate accelerate
acent accent
acept accept
ache [aching ached] achy
acheive achieve

achieve achievement
[achieving achieved]
acid acid rain

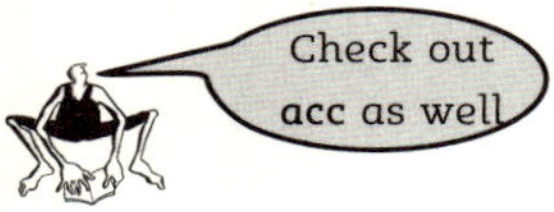

acident accident
acksel axel *[jump]
axil *[leaf]
axle *[wheel]
acne
acorn
acownt account
acre acreage
acrobat acrobatic
across
acselerate accelerate
acsent accent
acsept accept
acshun action
acsident accident
act [acting acted]
actchely actually
acter actor
action action-packed
active actively
activetys activities
activity activities

actor actress actresses
actual actually
acurate accurate
acuse accuse
acute acutely
ad *[advert] add *[sum]
Adam's apple
adapt [adapting adapted]
adaptable
add *[sum] ad *[advert]
[adding added]
addapt adapt
addenoyds adenoids
adder
addict [addicted] addiction
addition *[sum] edition *[copy]
additional
additive
addoor adore
address addresses
[addressing addressed]
ade aid
adenoids
ader adder
adhesive
adishun addition
adjective
adjust adjustable

admier admire

admiral

admire [admiring admired]

admiration

admit [admitting admitted]

admyre admire

adopt adoption

adorable

adore [adoring adored]

adress address

adult

advance

[advancing advanced]

advantage

advencher adventure

adventure adventurous

adverb

advertise

[advertising advertised]

advertisement

advice *[a tip] advise *[suggest]

advise *[suggest] advice *[a tip]

[advising advised]

advurb adverb

advurtise advertise

ael ale

aer air

aerial

aerodrome

aeroplane

aerosol

aery airy

afar *[long] affair *[event]

afect affect *[alter]

effect *[result]

affair

affect *[alter] effect *[result]

affection affectionate

affectionately

affekshun affection

afford affordable

affraede afraid

afid aphid

afloat

aford afford

afraid

after

afternoon

afterwards

aftr after

again

against

agane again

age [ageing aged]	
agectiv	adjective
agene	again
aggression	
aggressive aggressively	
agile	
ago	
agony agonies	
agre	agree
agree [agreeing agreed]	
agreeable	
agreement	
agreshun	aggression
agresiv	aggressive
agriculcher	agriculture
agriculture	
aground	
ahead	
aid [aiding aided]	
aim aimless aimlessly	
air *[gas]	heir *[inherits]
air-conditioning	
aircraft aircraft carrier	
airea	area
air ~fare ~field ~lift	
air ~line ~mail ~raid	
airial	aerial
airodrome	aerodrome
airoplane	aeroplane
airosol	aerosol
airport	
airy	
ais	ace
aisle *[passage]	isle *[island]
ajar	
ajective	adjective
ajile	agile
ajust	adjust
ake	ache

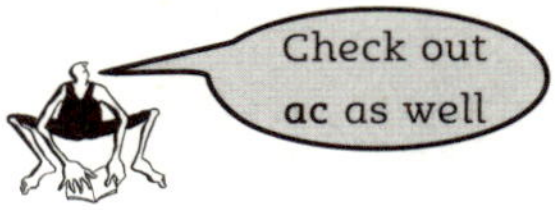

akselerayt	accelerate
akshun	action
aksident	accident
akt	act
aktiv	active
aktor	actor
Alah	Allah
alarm	
alastik	elastic
album	
alcohol alcoholic	
ale	
alein	alien
alert [alerting alerted]	

alevan	eleven
alfabet	alphabet
algae	
algebra	
algee	algae
alian	alien
alien	
aligator	alligator
alight	
alike	
alite	alight
aliterashun	alliteration
alive	
aljebra	algebra
alkaline	
alkohol	alcohol
all all right	
Allah	
allarm	alarm
allergic allergic reaction	
allergy allergies	
allert	alert
alley *[path]	ally *[friend]
alligator	
alliteration	
allmost	almost
allot *[give]	a lot *[many]
allotment	

allow [allowing allowed]	
allowed *[may]	aloud *[talk]
alltho	although
alltogether	altogether
allurgic	allergic
allwase	always
allways	always
ally *[friend]	alley *[path]
almond	
almost	
aloan	alone
alone	
along alongside	
a lot *[many]	allot *[give]
aloud *[talk]	allowed *[may]
alowed	allowed *[may]
	aloud *[talk]
alphabet alphabetical	
Alps alpine	
already	
Alsation	
also	
altar *[church]	
alter *[change] [altering altered]	
alteration	
alternative alternatively	
although	
althow	although

altitude
altogether
alurt alert
always
aly ally *[friend]
alley *[path]
alyke alike
alyve alive
am
amaze amazement
Amazon
ambassador
ambel amble
ambishun ambition
ambition
ambitious
amble [ambling ambled]
amboosh ambush
ambulance
ambush ambushes
ame aim
ameeba amoeba
amen
amethyst
amfibian amphibian
amfibious amphibious
ammaze amaze
ammunition
ammuse amuse
amoeba
among amongst
amount
amp
amphibian amphibious
amputate amputation
[amputating amputated]
amung among
amunishun ammunition
amuse amusement
amythist amethyst
an
anagram
anceint ancient
ancestor
anchor
ancient
ancor anchor
and
anemone
aneversary anniversary
anex annexe
aney any
angel *[God] angle *[maths]
angelic angelically
anger
angle *[maths] angel *[God]

angler
Anglo-Saxon
angree   angry
angrily
angry   angrier   angriest
angur   anger
angziety   anxiety
animal
animation
animel   animal
aniseed
aniversary   anniversary
anjel   angel
ankel   ankle
ankle
ankor   anchor
ankshus   anxious
anmils   animals
annalise   analyse
annexe
anniversary   anniversaries
annonymous   anonymous
annorak   anorak
annother   another
announce   announcement
annoy [annoying annoyed]
annual   annually
anonymous   anonymously

anorak
another
anownce   announce
anoy   annoy
ansed   answered
anser   answer
ansestor   ancestor
anshent   ancient
answer [answering answered]
ant *[insect]*   aunt *[family]*
Antarctic   Antarctica
antebyotic   antibiotic

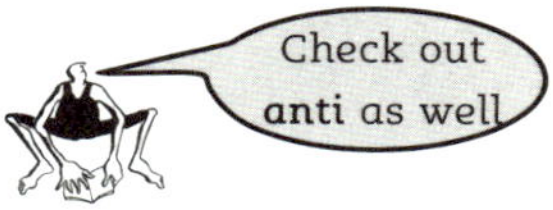

anteclimacks   anticlimax
anteek   antique
antehistameen   antihistamine
antelope
antenna   antennae
antesoshall   antisocial
anthology   anthologies
antibiotic
antic *[prank]*   antique *[old]*
anticeptic   antiseptic
anticlimax
anticlockwise
antihistamine

antilope — antelope
antique *[old] antic *[prank]
antiseptic
antisocial antisocially
antler
antonym
anual — annual
anuther — another
anuver — another
anxiety anxieties
anxious anxiously
any ~body ~how ~one
any ~thing ~way ~where
aorta
aparant — apparent
apart
ape

apeal — appeal
apear — appear
apel — apple
apetight — appetite
aphid
aplie — apply
aplikashun — application
aplord — applaud

apologetic
apologise
[apologising apologised]
apology apologies
apon — upon
apostrofee — apostrophe
apostrophe
appalling appallingly
apparatus
apparent apparently
apparition
appart — apart
appeal appealingly
appear [appearing appeared]
appearance
appendix appendicitis
appetising
appetite
applaud applause
[applauding applauded]
apple
application
apply [applying applied]
appolagise — apologise
appreciate appreciation
[appreciating appreciated]
approach approachable
[approaching approached]

approval
approve [approving approved]
Aprel April
apren apron
apricot
April April Fool's Day
aproch approach
apron
apruve approve
aquarium
Aquarius
Arab Arabian Arabic
arange arrange
arc *[curve] ark *[boat]
arcade
arch arches
archaeology archaeologist
archangel
archbishop
archer archery
archiology archaeology
architect architecture
archor archer
archway
Arctic Arctic Circle
are *[we are] our *[us]
area
areal aerial

arena
aren't *[are not] aunt *[family]
arest arrest
argew argue
argue
argument argumentative
argyoumont argument
arial aerial
arithmetic
arival arrival
arive arrive
ark *[boat] arc *[curve]
arkade arcade
arkangel archangel
arkiology archaeology
arkitect architect
Arktik Arctic
arm armchair
arma armour
armada
armadillo
armed forces
armie army
armond almond
armour armour-plated
army armies
arnt aren't *[are not]
aunt *[family]

arodrome aerodrome
arogant arrogant
aroplane aeroplane
arosol aerosol
around
arow arrow
arownd around
arrange
[arranging arranged]
arrangement
arrest [arresting arrested]
arrithmatic arithmetic
arrival
arrive [arriving arrived]
arrogant arrogantly
arrow arrow-head
arsen arson
arsenal
arsenic
arsk ask
arsnick arsenic
arson arsonist
art
artcher archer
arterie artery
artery arteries
arthritic arthritis
artic arctic

article
artificial artificially
artifishall artificial
artikal article
artist artistic
artrey artery
as *[compare] ass *[animal]
asassin assassin
asassinate assassinate
asc ask
ascape escape
ase ace
asembly assembly
asembul assemble
ash ashes ashen
ashamed
Ashun Asian
Asian
asist assist
ask [asking asked]
asleep
asma asthma
asortid assorted
asparagus
ass *[animal] as *[compare]
assassin assassination
assassinate
[assassinating assassinated]

assemble [assembling assembled]

assembly assemblies

assist [assisting assisted]

assistance assistant

assorted assortment

assume [assuming assumed]

Astec — Aztec

asterisk

asteroid

asthma asthmatic

astonish astonishment

astreisk — asterisk

astreoid — asteroid

astrologer

astronaut

astronomer astronomy

astronort — astronaut

asume — assume

at

atach — attach

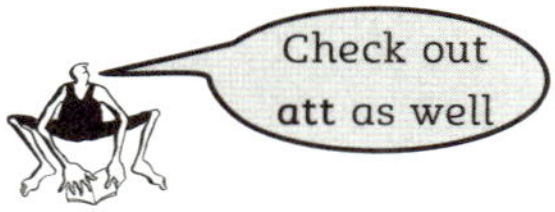

ate *[food] — eight *[number]

atempt — attempt

athlete athletic athletics

athority — authority

atic — attic

atishoo

atitude — attitude

Atlantic

atlas

atmosfere — atmosphere

atmosphere

atom atom bomb

atomic atomic energy

atract — attract

atractiv — attractive

attach [attaching attached]

attachment

attack [attacking attacked]

attempt [attempting attempted]

attend [attending attended]

attendance attendant

attention

attentive attentively

attic

attitude

attract [attracting attracted]

attraction attractive

atyshoo — atishoo

aubergine

auburn

auction auctioneer

audience

audishun — audition
audition
auditorium
auditory
auful — awful
August
aunt *[family] — ant *[insect]
aren't *[are not]
au pair
aural aurally
Aurgast — August
aut — out
author
authorisation authority
authorise
[authorising authorised]
autistic *[condition]
artistic *[skill]
autism
autobiography
autograph
automatic automatically
autopilot
autumn autumnal
avacado — avocado
avacouatid — evacuated
available availability
avalanche
avaleabul — available
avaperrat — evaporate
avapourate — evaporate
avary — aviary
avelanch — avalanche
avencherus — adventurous
avenew — avenue
aventure — adventure
avenue
average
averige — average
aviary aviaries
aviashun — aviation
aviation aviator
avlanch — avalanche
avocado
avoid [avoiding avoided]
avoyd — avoid
avrage — average
awair — aware
awake
award [awarding awarded]
aware awareness
away
awayk — awake
awdiense — audience
awful awfully
awght — ought

Awgust	August
awkward awkwardly	
awoke awoken	
awr	our
awt	ought
	out
awtumn	autumn
axe axes	
axel *[jump]	axle *[wheel]
axil *[leaf]	
axis axes	
axle *[wheel]	axel *[jump]
	axil *[leaf]
ayl	ale
aym	aim
ayt	eight *[number]
	ate *[food]
az	as

baa [baaing]	
babble [babbling babbled]	
babey	baby
babminton	badminton
baboon	
babul	babble
baby babyish	
babysit babysitter	
[babysitting babysat]	
bac	back
bace	base *[bottom]
	bass *[music]
bacen	bacon
bach	batch
bachelor	
back ~ache ~stroke ~wards	
backhand backhanded	
bacon	
bacteria bacterial	
bad badly badness	
bad worse worst	
baddy baddies	
badge	
badger	
badminton	
baffle [baffling baffled]	
bag bagpipes	
bagage	baggage

bage	badge
bager	badger
baggage	
baggy baggier baggiest	
baige	beige
baik	bake
bail *[out, cricket]	bale *[bundle]
bailiff	
bair	bare *[naked]
	bear *[carry, cub]
bairn	
bais	base *[bottom]
bait [baited]	
bak	back
bake [baking baked]	
bakery	
bakon	bacon
bakry	bakery
bakteria	bacteria
bal	ball *[kick]
balaclava	
balad	ballad
balance	
balcony	
bald *[head]	bawled *[cried]
	bold *[strong]
bale *[bundle]	bail *[out, cricket]
balense	balance

balerina ballerina

balkony balcony

ball *[kick] bawl *[cry]

ball

ballad

ballay ballet

ballerina

ballet

balloon balloonist

ballot

ballroom

balm

balmy *[mild] barmy *[mad]

baloon balloon

balot ballot

balune balloon

bamboo

bambu bamboo

ban [banning banned]

banana

band *[group, stripe]

banned *[stopped]

bandage

bandie bandy

bandige bandage

bandit

bandy bandy-legged

baned band *[group, stripe]

banned *[stopped]

baner banner

bang [banging banged]

bangle

banish banishment

banister

banjo

bank

bankrupt bankruptcy

bankwet banquet

bannana banana

banned *[stopped]

band *[group, stripe]

banner

bannish banish

bannister banister

banquet

banter

baonnet bayonet

baptise [baptising baptised]

baptism

bar *[pub] bare *[naked]

bar *[stop]

barage barrage

barax barracks

barb barbed
barbecue
barber
bare *[nude] bear *[cub]
bear *[carry]
bare barely
bare ~foot ~headed ~legged
barekaid barricade
barel barrel
baren baron *[noble]
barren *[dry]
bargain [bargaining bargained]
barge barge-pole
bargin bargain
baricade barricade
barier barrier
barister barrister
barje barge
bark
barley
barmaid barman
barmy *[mad] balmy *[mild]
barn
barnacle
barometer
baron *[noble] barren *[dry]
barracks
barrel

barren *[dry] baron *[noble]
barricade
barrier
barrister
barrow
barscit basket
barter [bartering bartered]
barth bath
bas base *[bottom]
bass *[music]
bascet basket
base *[bottom] bass *[music]
basement
bash [bashing bashed]
bashful bashfully
basic basically
basin basinful
basis bases
bask [basking basked]
basket basketball
basoon bassoon
bass *[music] base *[bottom]
bass-guitar bass-guitarist
bassoon bassoonist
baste [basting basted]
basyn basin
bat batsman
batalien battalion

batcheler	bachelor
baten	baton
bater	batter
batery	battery
bath *[tub]	
bathe *[swim] [bathing bathed]	
batik	
batrie	battery
battalion	
battel	battle
batter [battering battered]	
battery	
battle ~field ~ground	
batton	baton
battree	battery
batty battier battiest	
baul	ball *[sport, dance]
	bawl *[cry]
bawl *[cry]	ball *[kick]
bawt	bought
bay	
bayl	bale *[bundle]
	bail *[out, cricket]
bayliff	bailiff
bayonet	
bayt	bait
baything	bathing

bazaar	
bcos	because
be *[being]	bee *[insect]
beach *[sea]	beech *[tree]
beacon	
bead beady	
beaf	beef
beak beaker	
beam [beaming beamed]	
bean *[food]	been *[was]
beap	beep
bear *[cub]	bare *[naked]
beard bearded	
beast beastly	
beat [beating beaten]	
beautiful beautifully	
beauty *[lovely]	booty *[loot]
beaver	
became	
because	
beckon [beckoning beckoned]	
become [becoming became]	
becon	beckon
becos	because
becum	become
bed bed-linen	
bedlam	
Bedouin	

bedroom bedside

Bedwin Bedouin

bee *[insect] be *[being]

beech *[tree] beach *[sea]

beed bead

beef beefy

beefburger

beehive

beek beak

beem beam

been *[was] bean *[food]

beep [beeping beeped]

beer

beerd beard

beest beast

beestro bistro

beetle

beever beaver

befor before

before beforehand

befrend befriend

befriend [befriending befriended]

beg [begging begged]

beggar

begin [beginning began]

beginner

behave [behaving behaved]

behaviour

behead [beheading beheaded]

behed behead

behind

behvyer behaviour

beige

being

bekame became

bekause because

bekon beckon

bel bell

belated belatedly

belch [belching belched]

beleif belief

beleive believe

belfry belfries

belief

believe believable
[believing believed]

belive believe

bell bell-ringing

bellow *[yell] below *[under]

bellows

belly bellyache

belly-button belly-flop

belong [belonging belonged]

belongings

below *[under] bellow *[yell]

belt

bench benches	
bend [bending bent]	
beneath	
beneeth	beneath
benefit	
bent	
berbul	burble
berd	bird
berden	burden
bereaved bereavement	
bereeved	bereaved
beret *[hat]	berry *[fruit]
	bury *[cover]

berger	burger
berglar	burglar
bergul	burgle
berial	burial
berly	burly
bern	burn
bernt	burnt
berry *[fruit]	beret *[hat]
	bury *[cover]
berserk	
berst	burst
berth *[bunk]	birth *[born]
bery	berry *[fruit]
	bury *[cover]
beryed	buried
beseige	besiege
beside *[at the side]	
besides *[apart from]	
besiege [besieging besieged]	
besotted	
best	
bet [betting betted bet]	
betray [betraying betrayed]	
better	
between	
beuteful	beautiful
beware	
bewicht	bewitched
bewilder bewilderment [bewildering bewildered]	
bewitch [bewitching bewitched]	
beyond	
bhaji	
bi	by *[near]
	buy *[shop]
	bye *[farewell]
biannual	
bias biased biases	
bib	
Bible biblical	

biceps
bich bitch
bicker [bickering bickered]
bicos because
bicycle
bid [bidding bid]

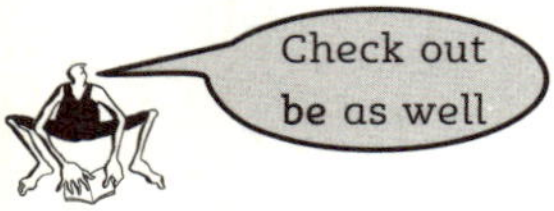

bifour before
big bigger biggest
bigan began
biger bigger
bigun begun
bihave behave
bihavior behaviour
bihind behind
bike
biker *[cyclist] bicker *[row]
bikini
bil bill
bilated belated
bilberry bilberries
bild billed *[invoiced]
build *[construct]
bilding building
bilevabul believable
bilingual

bilion billion
bill
billed *[pay] build *[house]
billiards
billion billionaire
billy goat
biloved beloved
bilow below
bilt built
bin *[box] been *[was]
bind binder binding
bineath beneath
binge
bingo
binoculars
biodegradable
biografer biographer
biographer biography
biological
biologist biology
bipass bypass
birch birches
bird bird-brained
birdbath birdseed
birden burden
birdie
bird's-eye view
birger burger

birgler burglar
birgul burgle
birnt burnt
Biro™
birth birthday
biscit biscuit
biscuit
biseige besiege
biseps biceps
bishop
biside beside
biskit biscuit
bison
bistro
bisycul bicycle
bit
bitch bitchy
bite *[teeth] byte *[data]
[biting bit bitten]
bite-size bite-sized
bitray betray
bitter bitterly
bitterness
bitween between
biware beware
biwilder bewilder
biy buy
biyond beyond

bizee busy
bizness business
blab [blabbing blabbed]
black ~bird ~board
black ~currant ~out ~smith
Black Death
blackberry blackberries
bladder
blade
blader *[skater] bladder *[urine]
blaid blade
blaim blame
blak black
blame blameless
blank blankly
blanket
blankit blanket
blare [blaring blared]
blarst blast
blast blast-off
blaze [blazing blazed]
blazer
bleach
bleak bleakly bleakness
bleat [bleating bleated]
bleech bleach
bleed [bleeding bled]
bleek bleak

bleep [bleeping bleeped]
bleet bleat
blend
bler blur
blert blurt
bless [blessing blessed]
blew *[wind] blue *[colour]
blind blindly blindness
blindfold blind-man's-buff
blink [blinking blinked]
blip
bliss blissful blissfully
blister
Blitz [the]
blizzard
blo blow
bloat [bloating bloated]
blob
bloch blotch
blochy blotchy
block [blocking blocked]
blockade
blockage
blod blood
blog [blogging blogged]
bloke
blonde
blong belong

blood ~curdling ~hound
blood ~shed ~shot ~stain
bloodthirsty
bloody
bloom [blooming bloomed]
blossom [blossoming blossomed]
blot [blotting blotted]
blotch blotches blotchy
blote bloat
blouse
blow [blowing blew blown]
blubber blubbery
blud blood
blue *[colour] blew *[wind]
bluebell bluebottle
bluff [bluffing bluffed]
bluish
blume bloom
blunder [blundering blundered]
blunt bluntly bluntness
blur [blurring blurred]
blurt [blurting blurted]
blush [blushing blushed]
bluwe blue
blynd blind
boa
boar *[pig] bore *[dull]
board *[wood] bored *[dull]

board [boarding boarded]
boast boastful
boat boating
bob bobsleigh
bobble
bobul bobble
boch botch
body bodies
bog boggy
bogel boggle
boggle [boggling boggled]
boggy
bogus
boil [boiling boiled]
boiler
boisterous boisterously
bok book
bolard bollard
bold *[strong] bald *[head]
bowled *[sport]
boldly
boler bowler
bolinase bolognaise
bollard
bolled bald *[head]
bold *[strong]
bowled *[sport]
bolognaise [spaghetti]

bolshy
bolt [bolting bolted]
bom bomb
bomb bomb-disposal
bomb ~shell ~site
bombard
[bombarding bombarded]
bomber
bommer bomber
bone
bonfire
Bonfire Night
bonkers
bonnet
bonus bonuses
bony bonier boniest
booby booby-prize
book ~case ~shelf ~shop
bookay bouquet
boom [booming boomed]
boomerang
boost [boosting boosted]
booster
boot
bootee *[shoe] booty *[loot]
booteek boutique
booth
booty *[loot] bootee *[shoe]

borbul bauble
border borderline
bordom boredom
bordor border
bore *[dull] boar *[pig]
bored *[dull] board *[wood]
boreding boarding
boredom
born *[birth]
borne *[carried]
borrow [borrowing borrowed]
bort bought
bosom
boss bossy
bost boast
botanist botany
botch [botching botched]
bote boat
botem bottom
both
bother [bothering bothered]
botom bottom
bottle bottle-feed
bottom bottomless
botul bottle
botum bottom
bough *[branch] bow *[bend]
bought *[buy] brought *[bring]

boukay bouquet
boulder *[rock] bolder *[braver]
bounce [bouncing bounced]
bouncy bouncier
bound [bounding bounded]
boundary boundaries
bounse bounce
bow *[bend] bough *[branch]
bow *[arrow, knot]
bow [bowing bowed]
bowel *[tummy]
bowl *[dish]
bowl *[action] [bowling bowled]
bowler
bowndree boundary
bownse bounce
box boxes
boxer
Boxing Day
boy *[male] buoy *[float]
boycott
boyfriend boyhood
boyish
boyl boil
Boy Scout
boystrus boisterous
bra bras
brace [bracing braced]

bracelet
bracken
bracket
brag [bragging bragged]
braid *[hair]   brayed *[ass]
braille
brain   brainwave
brainy   brainier   brainiest
brake *[slow]   break *[snap]
brake [braking braked]
braket   bracket
bramble
bran *[cereal]   brain *[mind]
branch   branches
brand   brand-new
brandish [brandishing brandished]
brane   brain
brar   bra
bras *[underwear]   brass *[metal]
braselet   bracelet
brash
brass   brassy
brat   brattish   brattishly
braul   brawl
brave   braver   bravest
bravery
brawd   broad
brawl

brawt   brought
bray [braying brayed]
braynee   brainy
bread *[food]   breed *[type]
break *[snap]   brake *[slow]
break [breaking broke broken]
break   ~neck ~through
breakfast
breast   breastbone
breath   breathy
breathe [breathing breathed]
breathless   breathlessly
breathtaking
breaze   breeze
brecfst   breakfast
bred *[animal]   bread *[food]
    breed *[type]
breed   breeder   breeding
breef   brief
breethe   breathe
breeze   breezy
breif   brief
brekfast   breakfast
brest   breast
breth   breath *[air]
    breathe *[in and out]
brethtaking   breathtaking

brew [brewing brewed]
brewed *[tea] brood *[kids]
brewery breweries
bribe [bribing bribed]
bribery
brick
bridal *[wedding] bridle *[horse]
bride ~groom ~smaid
bridge
bridle *[horse]
bridal *[wedding]
brief briefest briefly
brieze breeze
brigade
brige bridge
bright brighter brightest
brighten [brightening brightened]
brik brick
brilliance
brilliant brilliantly
brim
bring [bringing brought]
brisk briskly
bristle bristly
Britain *[place] Briton *[person]
brite bright
British
Briton *[person] Britain *[place]
Britten Britain
broad broader broadest
broaden [broadening broadened]
broadly
broak broke
broccoli
broch brooch
brocher brochure
brochure
brocoli broccoli
broke broken
brokn broken
bronse bronze
brontosaurus
bronze Bronze Age
brooch brooches
brood *[kids] brewed *[tea]
broody broodier broodiest
brook
broom broomstick
broose bruise
broot brute
brord broad
brort brought
brother brother-in-law
brought *[bring] bought *[buy]
brow
brown

brownie *[cake]

Brownie *[club]

browse [browsing browsed]

browser

brud   brood

brue   brew

bruise [bruising bruised]

brume   broom

brunch

brunette

brush   brushes

Brussels   brussels sprouts

brutal   brutally

brute   brutish

bruther   brother

brutle   brutal

brydal   bridal *[wedding]

bridle *[horse]

bryde   bride

bubble [bubbling bubbled]

bubbly

bucher   butcher

buck [bucking bucked]

bucket [bucketing bucketed]

Buckingham Palace

buckle   buckles

bud [budding budded]

Buddha

Buddhism   Buddhist

buddy   buddies

budge [budging budged]

budgerigar   budgie

budget [budgeting budgeted]

Budha   Buddha

bufalo   buffalo

buffalo   buffaloes

buffay   buffet

buffet *[food]

buffet *[wind] [buffeted]

bug [bugging bugged]

bugel   bugle

bugerigar   budgerigar

buget   budget

buggy   buggies

bugle

build *[construct] billed *[invoiced]

building

built   built-up

bujet   budget

bul   bull

bulb   bulbous

bulee   bully

bulge [bulging bulged]

bulit   bullet

bulitin   bulletin

bulj   bulge

bulk bulky
bull bullock
bull ~dog ~fight ~finch
bulldoze bulldozer
[bulldozing bulldozed]
bullet
bulletin
bullion
bully [bullying bullied]
bully bullies
bulrush bulrushes
buly bully
bumble [bumbling bumbled]
bumblebee
bumerang boomerang
bump [bumping bumped]
bumpy bumpier bumpiest
bun bunfight
bunch bunches
bundle [bundling bundled]
bung [bunging bunged]
bungalow
bungee
bungel bungle
bungie bungee
bungle [bungling bungled]
bunglo bungalow
bunjie bungee

bunk
bunker
bunny bunnies
Bunsen burner
bunsh bunch
buoy *[float] boy *[male]
burble [burbling burbled]
burch birch
burd bird
burden [burdening burdened]
burgeld burgled
burger
burglar
burglary burglaries
burgle *[rob] bugle *[horn]
burial
burly burlier burliest
burn [burning burned]
burnt
burp [burping burped]
burrow *[dig] borrow *[loan]
bursar bursary bursaries
burst [bursting burst]
bursurk berserk
burth berth *[bunk]
birth *[born]
bury *[cover] berry *[fruit]
bus buses

busel — bustle
bush bushes
bushy bushier bushiest
business businesses
business ~man ~woman
busker busking
bussel — bustle
bustle [bustling]
busy busier busiest
but *[however] — butt *[hit]
buten — button
buter — butter
butie — beauty *[lovely]
booty *[loot]
butiful — beautiful
butler
buton — button
butter buttery
butter ~cup ~fly ~scotch
buttock buttocks
button buttonhole

buty — beauty *[lovely]
booty *[loot]
buy *[shop] — bye *[goodbye]
by *[near]
buy [buying bought]
buzz [buzzes buzzing buzzed]
buzzard
bwuty — beauty
by *[near] — buy *[shop]
bye *[goodbye]
byceps — biceps

bycicul — bicycle
bye *[goodbye] — buy *[shop]
by *[near]
byer — buyer
bynoculars — binoculars
bypass bypasses
[bypassing bypassed]
byte *[data] — bite *[teeth]

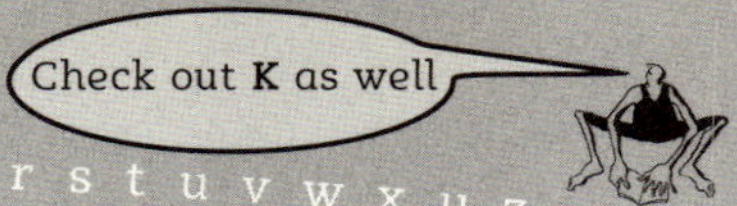

cab
cabale   cable
cabbage
cabin
cable
cackle [cackling cackled]
cactus   cacti
cadge [cadging cadged]
café *[snack]   coffee *[cup]
cage
caik   cake
caim   came
cair   care
caireful   careful
cake
calcium
calculate [calculating calculated]
calculation   calculator
calendar *[date]   colander *[food]
calf *[baby cow]   calves
calve *[give birth]
call [calling called]
calm   calmer   calmly
calorie   calories
calqulashun   calculation
calqulate   calculate
calqulator   calculator
calsium   calcium

calve *[give birth] carve *[cut]
[calving calved]
camaflarge   camouflage
came
camel
camelion   chameleon
camera   ~man
camouflage
camp   ~fire ~ground ~site
campaign
[campaigning campaigned]
camra   camera
can *[able, tin]   cane *[stick]
canal
canary   canaries
cancel [cancelling cancelled]
cancellation
cancer *[illness]
Cancer *[zodiac]
candel   candle
candle   ~light ~lit ~stick
candy   ~floss
cane
canibal   cannibal
cannibal   cannibalism
cannon   cannonball
cannot
canoe [canoeing canoed]

cansel — cancel

canser — cancer *[illness]

Cancer *[zodiac]

can't *[cannot]

canter [cantering cantered]

canue — canoe

canvas

canyon

cap *[hat, top] — cape *[cloak, land]

capable

capcher — capture

capillary capillaries

capital

Capricorn

capshun — caption

capsize [capsizing capsized]

capsule

captain

capten — captain

capter — captor

caption

captive captivity

capture [capturing captured]

car carsick

caracter — character

caramel

carat *[gold] — carrot *[food]

caravan caravanning

carbohydrate

carbon

carbord — cardboard

carcass carcasses

card cardboard

cardigan

cardinal

care carefree

caree — carry

career *[job] — carrier *[carries]

careful carefully

careless carelessly

carelessness

caretaker caretaking

cargo cargoes

Caribbean

carier — career *[job]

carrier *[carries]

carm — calm

carnation

carnival

carnivore carnivorous

carol carol-singing

carot — carat *[gold]

carrot *[food]

carpenter carpentry

carpet [carpeting carpeted]

carriage ~way
carrige carriage
carrot *[food] carat *[gold]
carry [carrying carried]
carsel castle
cart *[transport] kart *[go-kart]
cart ~horse ~load ~wheel
carten carton
carton *[box]
cartoon cartoonist
cartridge
cartune cartoon
carve *[cut] calve *[give birth]
[carving carved]
carving
caryon carrion
case [casing cased]
casel castle
caset cassette
cash *[money] catch *[ball]
casheltee casualty
cashew
cashier
cashmere
cashoe cashew
casino
casserole [casseroled]
cassette

cast castaway
caster *[sugar] castor *[oil, wheel]
castle
casual casually
casualty casualties
casum chasm
cat
catacomb catacombs
catalogue catalogues
catapult [catapulting catapulted]
catar catarrh
catarrh
catastrofee catastrophe
catastrophe catastrophic
catch [catching caught]
category categories
catekoom catacomb
catel cattle
catelog catalogue
catepolt catapult
cater [catering catered]
caterpillar
cathedral
Catholic Catholicism
catkin
catnap [catnapping catnapped]
cattle

caturpillar caterpillar
caught *[ball] court *[law]
cauldron
cauliflower
cause [causing caused]
caushun caution
caushus cautious
caution [cautioning cautioned]
cautious cautiously
cavalry
cave caveman
cavity cavities
cavurn cavern
caw *[crow] core *[centre]
corps *[army]
cawling calling
cawps corpse
cayg cage
caym came
cease *[stop] seize *[grab]

ceaseless ceaselessly
cedate sedate
ceeje siege
ceiling *[roof] sealing *[fastening]
celebrate celebration
[celebrating celebrated]
celebrity celebrities
celery
cell *[prison] sell *[shop]
cellabration celebration
cellar *[room] seller *[sales person]
cello cellist
Celsius
Celt Celtic
cement [cementing cemented]
cemetery cemeteries
cene scene *[theatre]
seen *[eyes]
cenile senile
census
cent *[money] scent *[smell]
sent *[away]
centaur
centenary
center centre
centigrade
centimetre
centipede
centir centre
central
centre [centring centred]

centry	sentry
centurion	
century centuries	
cenyer	senior
cep	keep
ceramic	
cerb	curb *[stop]
	kerb *[edge]
cercul	circle
cercus	circus
cereal *[grain]	serial *[sequence]
cerebral palsy	
ceremonial	
ceremony ceremonies	
cerf	serf *[slave]
	surf *[sea]
cerfew	curfew
cerial	cereal *[grain]
	serial *[sequence]
cerialise	serialise
cerkit	circuit
cername	surname
cerse	curse
cersor	cursor
certain *[sure]	curtain *[window]
certainty certainties	
certen	certain *[sure]
	curtain *[window]

certificate	
certsy	curtsy
cerve	curve
cesspit	
cew	cue *[signal]
	queue *[line]
chain [chaining chained]	
chair	
chaist	chased
chalet	
chalinge	challenge
chalk chalky	
challenge [challenging challenged]	
chamber	
chameleon	
champagne *[wine]	campaign *[activity]
champion championship	
chance chances chancy	
chandelier	
chane	chain
change [changing changed]	
changeable	
chanj	change
channel [channelling]	
Channel [the English]	
chanse	chance
chant [chanting chanted]	

chaos chaotic
chap
chapati
chapel chaplain
chaplin chaplain
chapter
chapul chapel
character characteristic
charade
charcoal
chare chair
charge [charging charged]
chariot charioteer
charitable
charity charities
charm [charming charmed]
charnce chance
charnt chant
chart [charting charted]
charter flight
chase [chasing chased]
chasm chasms
chat [chatting chatted]
chateau
chatter [chattering chattered]
chatty chattier
chauffeur
chaw chore

cheap *[money] cheep *[bird]
cheap cheaper cheaply
cheat [cheating cheated]
check *[inspect] cheque *[money]
[checking checked]
checkmate
Cheddar cheese
cheef chief
cheeften chieftain
cheek
cheeky cheekier cheekiest
cheep *[bird] cheap *[money]
cheepen cheapen
cheer [cheering cheered]
cheerful cheerfully
cheerfulness
cheese ~burger ~cake
cheesy cheesier cheesiest
cheetah
chef *[cook] chief *[boss]
cheir chair
chello cello
chemical chemically
chemist chemistry
cheque *[money] check *[inspect]
cherch church
chere chair
cheree cherry

cherish [cherishes] [cherishing cherished]
chern — churn
cherry cherries
cherub cherubic
chess chessboard
chest chesty
chestnut
chew [chewing chewed]
chews *[food] — choose *[pick]
chewy chewier chewiest
chick
chicken chickenpox
chickpea
chief chiefs chiefly
chieftain
chier — cheer
chiffon
chilblain
child children childish
chill [chilling chilled]
chilli *[food] chillis
chilly *[cold] chillier
chime [chiming chimed]
chimney chimneys
chimp chimpanzee
chin chinless
china *[cup] — China *[place]

chinchilla
Chinese
chink
chip [chipping chipped]
chipmunk
chipolata
chirp [chirping chirped]
chirpy chirpier chirpiest
chisel [chiselling chiselled]
chivalry chivalrous
chloride
chlorine
chlorophyll
chocerlit — chocolate
chocolate
chofer — chauffeur
choice
choir
choke [choking choked]
cholera
cholesterol
choose *[pick] — chews *[food] [choosing chose chosen]
choosy choosier choosiest
chop [chopping chopped]
chopsticks
choppy choppier choppiest
choral

chord *[music]   cord *[rope]
chore
chork   chalk
chortle [chortling chortled]
chorus   choruses
choys   choice
Christ
christal   crystal
christen [christening christened]
Christian   Christianity
Christmas
chriy   try
chrome
chromosome
chronic
chronicle
chronological
chrysalis   chrysalises
chrysanthemum
chrystallise   crystallise
chubby   chubbier   chubbiest
chuck [chucking chucked]
chuckle [chuckling chuckled]
chue   chew
chug [chugging chugged]
chum   chummy   chummier
chunk   chunky   chunkier
church   churches

churn [churning churned]
churp   chirp
chuse   choose
chute *[slide]   shoot *[target]
chyna   china
cianide   cyanide
cichin   kitchen
ciclist   cyclist
ciclone   cyclone
cicul   cycle
cider
ciense   science
cientific   scientific
cigar   cigarette
cignet   cygnet *[swan]
    signet *[ring]
cilindar   cylinder
cimbal   cymbal *[music]
    symbol *[sign]
cinder
cinema
cinus   sinus
circit   circuit
circle
circuit
circular
circulate   circulation
[circulating circulated]

circumference
circumstance
circus circuses
cissors scissors

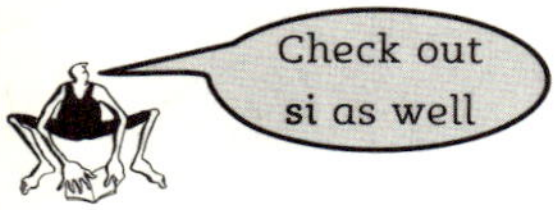

cissy cissies
cist cyst
citadel
cite *[quote] sight *[seeing]
[citing cited] site *[place]
citee city
citizen citizenship
citrus
city cities
civil civilian
civilisation
civilise [civilising civilised]
clad
claim [claiming claimed]
clairvoyant
clam
clamber [clambering clambered]
clame claim
clammy clammier
clamp [clamping clamped]
clan

clang [clanging clanged]
clank [clanking clanked]
clap [clapping clapped]
clarinet clarinettist
clarss class
clash [clashes clashing clashed]
clasik classic
clasp [clasping clasped]
class classes
class ~room ~work
classic classical
clatter [clattering clattered]
clause *[part] claws *[animal]
claustrophobia
claustrophobic
claw [clawing clawed]
claws *[animal] clause *[part]
clay
clean [cleaning cleaned]
cleanliness cleanly
cleanse [cleansing cleansed]
clear [clearing cleared]
clear clearly
cleen clean
cleer clear
cleeshay cliché
clementine
clench [clenching clenched]

clense cleanse
clergy
clever cleverer cleverest
cleverly cleverness
clew clue
cliché
client
cliff cliffhanger
clik click
clim climb
climate climatic
climax climaxes
climb [climbing climbed]
climed climbed
climing climbing
cling [clinging clung]
clinic
clink [clinking clinked]
clip [clipping clipped]
cloak cloakroom
clobber [clobbering clobbered]
clock clockwork
clockwatch [clockwatches]
clog [clogged]
cloke cloak
clone
clorafill chlorophyll
clore claw
cloride chloride
clorinate chlorinate
clorine chlorine
clorofill chlorophyll
clors clause *[part]
claws *[animal]
clorstrofobia claustrophobia
close [closing closed]
close closer closest
closely closeness
closet
clot [clotting clotted]
cloth *[material]
clothe *[put clothes on]
clothes clothing
cloud cloudless
cloudy cloudier cloudiest
clout [clouting clouted]
clove
clover
clowd cloud
clown clownish
clowt clout
club [clubbing clubbed]
cluch clutch
cluck [clucking clucked]
clue clueless
clump [clumping clumped]

clumpy clumpier clumpiest
clumsy clumsier clumsiest
clunk [clunking clunked]
clurgy clergy
cluster [clustering clustered]
clutch clutches
[clutching clutched]
clutter [cluttering cluttered]
clyent client
clyme climb
coach coaches
[coaching coached]
coal coalmine
coarse coarsely
coast ~guard ~line
coastal
coat
cobble cobblestone
[cobbling cobbled]
cobra
cobweb
Coca Cola™
coch coach
cock cock-a-doodle-doo
cockatoo
cockerel
cockney
cockpit

cockroach cockroaches
cocky cockier cockiest
cocoa
coco cocoa
coconut
cocoon [cocooning cocooned]
cocune cocoon
cod
code
coed could
coff cough
coffee *[cup] café *[snack]
coffin
cohort
coil [coiling coiled]
coin [coining coined]
coincidence
cokatoo cockatoo
cola *[drink] collar *[neck]
colander *[food] calendar *[time]
colaps collapse
cold colder coldest
coldly coldness
cole coal
coleeg colleague
coler collar *[neck]
colour *[red]
colera cholera

colerbone collarbone
colerful colourful
coleslaw
colesterol cholesterol
colide collide
colige college
collage
collapse collapsible
[collapsing collapsed]
collar collarbone
collarj collage
colleague
collecshun collection
collect collector
[collecting collected]
collection
college
collide [colliding collided]
colliflower cauliflower
collision
colloquial
collum column
colon
colonel *[army] kernel *[seed]
colony colonies
coloqueal colloquial
colour colourless
colourful colourfully

column
coma *[sleep] comma *[text]
comando commando
comb
combat
combine combination
[combining combined]
come [coming came]
comedian comedy comedies
comeing coming
comemorate commemorate
comen common
comense commence
coment comment
comentry commentary
comershal commercial
comet *[sky] commit *[to do]
comforball comfortable
comfort [comforting comforted]
comfortable comfortably
comfy
comic comical
comidian comedian
coming
comit comet *[sky]
commit *[to do]
comitee committee
comma *[text] coma *[sleep]

command commander
[commanding commanded]
commando
commemorate
commence
[commencing commenced]
comment commentator
[commenting commented]
commentary commentaries
commer comma
commercial commercially
commic comic
commit *[to do] comet *[sky]
commit commitment
[committing committed]
committee
common commonly
Commonwealth Games
commotion
communicate
[communicating communicated]
communication
communism communist
community communities
commute commuter
[commuting commuted]
comon common
comoshun commotion

compact
compair compare
companion
company companies
companyon companion
compare comparison
[comparing compared]
compartment
compashun compassion
compass compasses
compassion compassionate
compeet compete
compensate compensation
[compensating compensated]
compete competitor
[competing competed]
competent competently
competition competitive
compitishun competition
complain complaint
[complaining complained]
complane complain
compleks complex
complekshun complexion
complete completely
[completing completed]
complex
complexion

complicate complication
[complicating complicated]
compliment complimentary
compose [composing composed]
compost
compound
comprehend
[comprehending comprehended]
comprehension
comprehensive
comprihenshun comprehension
compulsion compulsive
compulsory
computer
comunicate communicate
comunism communism
comunitee community
comute commute
con [conning conned]
concave
conceal [concealing concealed]
conceit [conceited]
concensus consensus
concentrate concentration
[concentrating concentrated]
concepshun conception
concept
conception

concequense consequence
concern [concerning concerned]
concert
concienshus conscientious
concious conscious
concise concisely
concist consist
concistency consistency
conclewd conclude
conclude conclusion
[concluding concluded]
concoct concoction
[concocting concocted]
concrete
concussed concussion
condem condemn
condemn condemnation
[condemning condemned]
condense condensation
[condensing condensed]
condishun condition
condition conditional
conditioner
conduct conductor
[conducting conducted]
cone
conference
conferm confirm

confess confession
[confessing confessed]
confest confessed
confetti
confide confidence
[confiding confided]
confident confidently
confidential confidentially
confine [confined]
confirm confirmation
[confirming confirmed]
confiscate confiscation
[confiscating confiscated]
conflict
confrence conference
confront confrontation
[confronting confronted]
confuse confusion
[confusing confused]
confyde confide
congrachulate congratulate
congratulate
[congratulating congratulated]
congratulations
conical
conifer coniferous
conjer conjure
conjunction

conjure conjuror
[conjuring conjured]
conkave concave
conker *[nut] conquer *[win]
conkrete concrete
conkussed concussed
conkwest conquest
connect connection
[connecting connected]
conquer *[win] conker *[nut]
conqueror conquest
conscience
conscientious
conscientiously
conscious consciously
conseat conceit
consecutive consecutively
conseel conceal
conseive conceive
consensus
consent [consenting consented]
consentrashun concentration
consentrate concentrate
consept concept
consequence
consern concern
consert concert
conservation

conservative
conservatory
conserve [conserving conserved]
conshense conscience
conshienshus conscientious
conshus conscious
consider considerable
[considering considered]
considerate consideration
consise concise
consist [consisting consisted]
consistent consistently
consolation prize
console [consoling consoled]
consonant
conspiracy conspiracies
constable
constant
constellation
constipated constipation
construcshun construction
construct construction
[constructing constructed]
constructive constructively
consult consultant
[consulting consulted]
consume consumer
[consuming consumed]
consurlashun consolation
consurvashun conservation
consurvativ conservative
consurvatory conservatory
consyoum consume
contact [contacting contacted]
contagious
contain container
[containing contained]
contajus contagious
contaminate contamination
[contaminating contaminated]
contane contain
contemplate contemplation
[contemplating contemplated]
contemporary
contemporaries
contempt
content contentment
contest contestant
[contesting contested]
context
continent *[land mass]*
Continent *[the]*
continual continually
continuation
continue continuity
[continuing continued]

continuous continuously
contour
contract contractor
[contracting contracted]
contradict contradiction
[contradicting contradicted]
contraption
contrary
contrast [contrasting contrasted]
contredict — contradict
contrery — contrary
contribute contributor
[contributing contributed]
contribution
control controllable
[controlling controlled]
controversy controversial
convay — convey
convayer belt — conveyor belt
convecshun — convection
convection convector
conveks — convex
convenient conveniently
convent
conversation
conversion
convert convertible
[converting converted]
convex
convey [conveying conveyed]
conveyor belt
convict conviction
[convicting convicted]
convince [convincing convinced]
convinient — convenient
convinse — convince
convoy
convulse [convulsed]
convulsion
convursashun — conversation
convurshun — conversion
convurt — convert
cood — could
cook cooker
[cooking cooked]
cookery
cool cooler coolest
coolly
co-operate co-operation
[co-operating co-operated]
co-operative
co-operatively
co-ordinashun — co-ordination
co-ordinate co-ordinator
[co-ordinating co-ordinated]
co-ordination

cop *[get] [copping copped]
cope *[deal with] [coping coped]
copie   copy
co-pilot
copper
copy copies [copying copied]
coral *[sea]   choral *[sing]
Coran   Koran
cord *[rope]   chord *[music]
corduroy
core *[centre]   caw *[crow]
    corps *[army]
corel   choral *[sing]
    coral *[sea]
corespond   correspond
corght   caught *[ball]
    court *[law]
corige   courage
corjet   courgette
cork corkscrew
corldron   cauldron
corled   called
cormorant
corn corn-on-the-cob
corner
cornet
corny
corode   corrode

corporal
corprel   corporal
corps *[army]
corpse *[body]
corral *[pen]   coral *[sea]
correct correction
[correcting corrected]
correspond correspondence
[corresponding corresponded]
corridor
corroad   corrode
corrode [corroding corroded]
corrugated iron
cors   cause *[reason]
    course *[order, path]
corse   cause *[reason]
    coarse *[rough]
    course *[order, path]
corshun   caution
cort   caught *[ball]
    court *[law]
cortier   courtier
cortmarshall   court-martial
coschume   costume
cosee   cosy
cosmetic

cosmonaut
cost *[value] coast *[sea]
cost costly
coste coast
costume
cosy cosier cosiest
cot *[bed] coat *[clothing]
coton cotton
cottage
cotton
couch couches
cough
could couldn't [could not]
counsellor
count counter
[counting counted]
countess
country countries
county counties
couple
couplet
courage
courageous courageously
courd cord *[rope]
chord *[music]
courgette
courier
course *[meal] coarse *[rough]

coursework
court *[law] caught *[ball]
courteous courteously
courtesy *[polite] curtsy *[bow]
court-martial
cousin
cove
cover [covering covered]
cow ~boy ~girl ~slip
coward
cowardly cowardice
cowch couch
cownsel council *[assembly]
counsel *[advise]
[counselling counselled]
cownseller counsellor *[adviser]
cownt count
coyn coin
cozmetic cosmetic
cozmic cosmic
cozmonort cosmonaut
crab crabby
crack [cracking cracked]
crackle [crackling crackled]
cradle [cradling cradled]
craft craftsman

crafty craftier craftiest

crag craggy

craip crepe *[paper]
crêpe *[pancake]

craizee crazy

crak crack

crakul crackle

cram [cramming crammed]

cramp [cramping cramped]

cranberry cranberries

crane [craning craned]

crank [cranking cranked]

cranky crankier crankiest

crash *[accident] crashes
crush *[squash]

crash [crashes crashing crashed]

crate *[box]

crater *[large hole]

crawl [crawling crawled]

crayon

craze crazy crazier

creacher creature

creak creaky

cream creamy

creap creep

crease [creasing creased]

create creator creation
[creating created]

creative creatively

creativity

creature

crèche

crecher creature

credit [credited]

creem cream

creep creeper creepy
[creeping crept]

creese crease

cremation crematorium

crepe *[paper]

crêpe *[pancake]

crepey creepy

crept

crescent

cress

cressent crescent

crevasse *[ice]

crevice *[crack]

crew

criashun creation

criate create

criativ creative

crib

cricket cricketer

crie cry

cried

crikit cricket
crime
criminal
crimson
cringe [cringing cringed]
crinj cringe
crinkle crinkly
cript crypt
crisis crises
crisp crispy crispier
crissen christen
Crist Christ
cristal crystal
criteria
critic critical critically
criticise criticism
[criticising criticised]
critisize criticise
croak croaky croakier
[croaking croaked]
crock crockery
crocodile
crocus crocuses
crokay croquet
croke croak
crokodile crocodile
crokus crocus
crome chrome

crook crooked
crop [cropping cropped]
croquet
crorl crawl
cross crosser crossly
cross ~roads ~word
crouch [crouching crouched]
croud crowd
crow [crowing crowed]
crowch crouch
crowd *[people]*
crowed *[cockerel]*
crowkay croquet
crown [crowning crowned]
cruch crutch
crucified crucifix
crude crudely
crue crew
cruel crueller
cruelly cruelty
cruise *[trip]* crews *[teams]*
crumb crumbly
crumble *[break]*
[crumbling crumbled]
crumple *[crease]* [crumpled]
crunch crunchy crunchier
[crunching crunched]
crusade crusader

crush [crushing crushed]

crust crusty

crutch crutches

cry cries

cry [cries crying cried]

crysalis chrysalis

crysanthemum chrysanthemum

crystal

cryticysum criticism

cub

cube cuboid

cubicle

cubord cupboard

cuckoo

cucumber

cud

cuddle cuddly [cuddling cuddled]

cue *[signal] queue *[line]

cuff cufflink

culcher culture

cule cool

cull [culling culled]

culla colour

culprit

cultivate cultivator [cultivating cultivated]

cultivation

culture cultural

cum come

cumfertabul comfortable

cumfort comfort

cumfy comfy

cumpanee company

cumpass compass

cunning cunningly

cuntree country

cup cupful cuppa

cupboard

Cupid

cuple couple

curb *[stop] kerb *[edge]

cure [curing cured]

curensy currency

curent currant *[fruit] current *[flow, now]

curfew

curier courier

curiosity

curious curiously

curl [curling curled]

curly curlier

currage courage

currant *[fruit] current *[flow, now]

currency   currencies

current *[flow, now]   currant *[fruit]

current   currently

curriculum

curry   curries

curse [cursing cursed]

cursive

cursor

curtain *[net]   certain *[sure]

curtificate   certificate

curtsy *[bow]   courtesy *[polite]

curve [curving curved]

cury   curry

cushion

cusin   cousin

custard

custody

custom   customer

cut *[with a knife]   cutter [cutting cut]

cute *[sweet] cuter   cutest

cutlery

cuver   cover

cyanide

cyberspace

cycle [cycling cycled]

cyclist

cyclone   cyclonic

cygnet *[swan]   signet *[ring]

cylinder   cylindrical

cymbal *[music]   symbol *[sign]

cymbolic   symbolic

cynonim   synonym

cyringe   syringe

cyrup   syrup

cystem   system

cyte   sight

czar   czarina

D-Day
dab [dabbing dabbed]
dabble [dabbling dabbled]
dabel — dabble
Dachshund
dad daddy daddies
daffodil
daft dafter daftest
dagger
daily
dair — dare
dairy *[milk] — diary *[book]
daisy daisies
Dalmashun — Dalmatian
Dalmatian
dam *[water] — damn *[curse]
damage [damaging damaged]
dame
damige — damage
damn *[curse] — dam *[water]
[damning damned]
damp dampness
dampen [dampening dampened]
damson
dance [dancing danced]
dandelion
dandruff
dandylion — dandelion
danger dangerous
dangerously
dangle [dangling dangled]
dangros — dangerous
danjer — danger
dank
dans — dance
dapple [dappling dappled]
dare [daring dared]
darey — dairy
dark darkly darkness
darken [darkening darkened]
darling
darn [darning darned]
dart [darting darted]
dash dashes [dashing dashed]
data database
date [dating dated]
daughter
daun — dawn
dauter — daughter
dawdle dawdler
[dawdling dawdled]
dawn [dawning dawned]
daxhound — Dachshund
day ~break ~dream ~light
dayity — deity
dayly — daily

days *[dates] daze *[stun]
dayt date
daze *[stun] days *[dates]
dazzle [dazzling dazzled]
dead *[not alive] deed *[action]
deaden [deadening deadened]
deadly deadlier
deaf deafness
deafen [deafening deafened]
deafeningly
deal [dealing dealt]
dealer dealership
dealt
dear *[loved] deer *[animal]
dearest dearly
death deathly
debait debate
debatable
debate [debating debated]
debt debtor
decade *[10 years] decayed *[rotted]
decarate decorate
decay [decaying decayed]
deceit deceitful
deceitfully deceitfulness
deceive [deceiving deceived]
December

decent *[good] descent *[down]
decently
deception
deceptive deceptively
decibel
decide [deciding decided]
decidedly
deciduous
decimal
decipher [deciphering deciphered]
decision
deck [decking decked]
declaration
declare [declaring declared]
decline [declining declined]
decode [decoding decoded]
decomposed
decorate decorator [decorating decorated]
decoration
decorative decoratively
decoy
decrativ decorative
decrease decreasingly [decreasing decreased]
decree *[law] degree *[uni]
ded dead *[not alive] deed *[action]

dedicate dedication
[dedicating dedicated]
deduct deduction
[deducting deducted]
deed *[action] dead *[not alive]
deel deal
deep deeply
deepen [deepening deepened]
deepfreeze deep-frozen
deer *[animal] dear *[loved]
deezel diesel
def deaf
defeat [defeating deafeated]
defect
defence defenceless
defend defendant
[defending defended]
defens defence
defensive defensively
deffen deafen
defiant defiantly
define [defining defined]
definetly definitely
definishun definition
definite definitely
definition
deform [deformed]
deformity deformities

defrost [defrosting defrosted]
defuse [defusing defused]
defy [defies defying defied]
degree *[uni] decree *[law]
dehydrate [dehydrated]
de-ice [de-icing de-iced]
deity deities
deject [dejected] dejection
dek deck
dekorate decorate
delay [delaying delayed]
delete deletion [deleting deleted]
deliberate deliberately
[deliberating deliberated]
delicacy delicacies
delicate delicately
delicatessen
delicious deliciously
delight [delighting delighted]
delightful delightfully
delinquent delinquency
delishus delicious
deliver deliverer
[delivering delivered]
delivery deliveries
delt dealt
deluge [deluged]
demand [demanding demanded]

demented dementia
demerara
demist [demisting demisted]
demo
democratic democratically
demolish [demolishes]
[demolishing demolished]
demolition
demon demonic
demonstrate demonstration
[demonstrating demonstrated]
demoralise
[demoralising demoralised]
den
dencher denture
denial
denim
denomination denominator
dense *[thick] dents *[dips]
density
dent [denting dented]
dental
dentist denture
deny [denies denying denied]
denyal denial
deodorant
depart departure
[departing departed]

department
depend dependable
[depending depended]
dependence dependent
depict [depicting depicted]
depo depot
deport [deporting deported]
deportation
deposit
depot
depress depression
[depressing depressed]
deprive deprivation
[depriving deprived]
depth
deputy
derail [derailing derailed]
derelict
dert dirt
descant
descend descendant
[descending descended]
descent *[down] decent *[good]
descrete discreet
describe [describing described]
description descriptive
deseet deceit
Desember December

desent decent
desert *[sand] dessert *[food]
desert *[leave] desertion
deserve deservedly
[deserving deserved]
desibell decibel
deside decide
desifer decipher
design designer
[designing designed]
desimal decimal
desirable
desire [desiring desired]
desk
despair despairingly
[despairing despaired]
desperashun desperation
desperate desperately
desperation
despise [despising despised]
despite
deposit [depositing deposited]
despute dispute
dessend descend
dessent decent *[good]
descent *[down]
dessert *[food] desert *[sand]
desert *[leave]

destination
destiny [destined]
destroy destroyer
[destroying destroyed]
destruction
destructive destructively
det debt
detail [detailing detailed]
detain [detaining detained]
detect [detecting detected]
detectable detection
detector detective
detention
deter deterrant
[deterring deterred]
detergent
deteriate deteriorate
deteriorate deterioration
[deteriorating deteriorated]
determination
determine determined
detest detestable
[detesting detested]
deth death
detonate detonator
[detonating detonated]
detour
deuce

devastate devastation	
[devastating devastated]	
develop development	
[developing developed]	
device *[thing]	devise *[invent]
devide	divide
devil	
devious deviously	
devise *[invent]	device *[thing]
devorse	divorce
devoshun	devotion
devote [devoting devoted]	
devotion	
devour [devouring devoured]	
devout devoutly	
devyce	device *[thing]
	devise *[invent]
dew *[drops]	Jew *[religion]
	due *[owing]
dewet	duet
dewy	
diabetes diabetic	
diafram	diaphragm
diagnose [diagnosed]	
diagnosis diagnoses	
diagonal diagonally	
diagram	
dial [dialling dialled]	

dialect	
dialogue	
diameter	
diamond	
diaphragm	
diar	dire *[bad]
	dear *[loved]
	deer *[animal]
diarrhoea	
diarria	diarrhoea
diary *[book]	dairy *[milk]
dibate	debate

dice	
diceive	deceive
dicree	decree
dicshunry	dictionary
dictate dictation	
[dictating dictated]	
dictator dictatorship	
dictionary dictionaries	
did *[do]	died *[die]
dide	died
dident	didn't
didn't [did not]	
diduct	deduct

die *[death]	dye *[colour]
[dies dying died]	
died *[death]	did *[do]
	dyed *[colour]
diesel	
diet [dieting dieted]	
difend	defend
differ [differing differed]	
different differently	
difficult	
difficulty difficulties	
difrens	difference
difrent	different
dify	defy
dig [digging dug]	
digest [digesting digested]	
digestion digestive	
digit digital digitally	
dignify dignified	
dignity	
digraph	
digree	degree
diing	dyeing *[colour]
	dying *[about to die]
dijestshun	digestion
dijital	digital
dikshunrey	dictionary

diktater	dictator
dilapidated	
dilay	delay
dilect	dialect
dilemma	
dilete	delete
diling	dialling
dilinquent	delinquent
dilishus	delicious
dilute [diluting diluted]	
dimand	demand
dimensha	dementia
dimension	
dimentid	demented
diminish [diminishing diminished]	
dimple [dimpled]	
din	
dinasty	dynasty
dinatime	dinner time
dine [dining dined]	
dinghy *[boat]	dingy *[dull]
dingo dingoes	
dingy *[dull]	dinghy *[boat]
dinial	denial
dinner	
dinosaur	
diodorant	deodorant
dioxide	

dip [dipping dipped]
dipacher departure
dipart depart
diploma
diplomacy
diplomat diplomatic
diposzit deposit
dire
direct [directing directed]
direction directly
directness director
directory directories
dirt dirty dirtier
disability disabilities
disable disabled
disadvantage
disagree disagreeable
disagreed disagreement
disappear disappearance
[disappearing disappeared]
disappoint disappointment
[disappointing disappointed]
disapproval
disapprove
[disapproving disapproved]
disarm [disarming disarmed]
disaster disastrous
disastrously

disbelief
disc *[circle, music]
disk *[computer]
discend descend
discharge [discharging discharged]
disciple
discipline disciplined
disco discotheque
discomfort
disconnect [disconnected]
discontented
discotech discotheque
discount [discounted]
discourage discouragement
[discouraging discouraged]
discover discovery
[discovering discovered]
discreet discreetly
discribe describe
discriminate discrimination
[discriminating discriminated]
discripshun description
discurige discourage
discus *[throw]
discuss *[talk] discussion
[discussing discussed]
disease diseased
disect dissect

disembark [disembarking disembarked]

disepshun	deception
diseptiv	deceptive
disert	desert *[leave]
	dessert *[food]
diserve	deserve
diseve	deceive

disgrace [disgracing disgraced]

disgraceful disgracefully

disgruntled

disguise [disguised]

disgust [disgusting disgusted]

dish dishes

dishevelled

dishonest dishonestly

dishonesty

diside	decide
disiduus	deciduous

disillusion [disillusioned]

disine	design

disinfect disinfectant [disinfecting disinfected]

disintegrate disintegration [disintegrating disintegrated]

disirabul	desirable
disire	desire

disjointed

disk *[computer] disc *[circle, music]

diskomfort	discomfort
dislexsia	dyslexia

dislike [disliked]

dislodge [dislodged]

disloyal

dismal dismally

dismiss dismissal [dismissing dismissed]

disobedience disobedient

disobey [disobeying disobeyed]

disorder disorderly

disorganise [disorganised]

disorganisation

disorientated

disown [disowning disowned]

dispair	despair

dispatch dispatches [dispatching dispatched]

disperse [dispersed]

dispise	despise
dispite	despite

display [displaying displayed]

displeased

dispose [disposing disposed]

disposable disposal

dispraxia	dyspraxia

disprove *[deny] disapprove *[bad]
dispute [disputing disputed]
disqualification
disqualify disqualifies [disqualifying disqualified]
disregard [disregarded]
disrespectful disrespectfully
disrupt disruption [disrupting disrupted]
disruptive disruptively
dissapear — disappear
dissapoint — disappoint
disscurrage — discourage
dissect dissection [dissecting dissected]
dissendent — descendant
dissert — desert *[leave]; dessert *[food]
dissiplin — discipline
dissolve [dissolving dissolved]
dissproov — disprove
distance
distant distantly
distilled distillery
distinct distinctly
distinction
distinctive distinctively
distinguish [distinguishes] [distinguishing distinguished]
distort distortion [distorting distorted]
distract distraction [distracting distracted]
distress [distresses] [distressing distressed]
distribute [distributing distributed]
distribution distributor
district
distroy — destroy
distructiv — destructive
distrust distrustful [distrusting distrusted]
disturb disturbance [disturbing disturbed]
disused
disyfer — decipher
ditch ditches [ditching ditched]
ditectiv — detective
ditenshun — detention
diter — deter
ditermin — determine
ditest — detest
dither [dithering dithered]
dive [diving dived]
divelop — develop

diversion
divert [diverting diverted]
divice device
divide [dividing divided]
divine divinely
divisible
division divisor
divorce [divorcing divorced]
divurtid diverted
dizease disease
dizzy dizzier dizziest
dlishus delicious
do *[act] doe *[deer]
do [does doing did]
dock [docking docked]
doctor
document documentary
[documenting documented]
doddery
dodge [dodging dodged]
dodgy dodgier
dodgem
doe *[deer] dough *[bread]
does doesn't [does not]
dog dogged doggy
doj dodge
dojem dodgem
dokter doctor

dole [doling doled]
dolfin dolphin
doll dolly dollies
dollar
dollop
dolphin
dome *[shape] doom *[gloom]
Domesday Book
domestic
dominance dominant
dominate domination
[dominating dominated]
domino dominoes
donate donation
[donating donated]
done
donkey donkeys
donor
don't [do not]
doodle [doodling doodled]
doom [doomed]
Doomsday Domesday *[Book]
door doorknob
dooy do
dope dopey
dordul dawdle
dormitory dormitories
dormouse dormice

dorn dawn

dorter daughter

dosage

dose *[medicine] does *[do]

doze *[nap]

dotty dottier

double [doubling doubled]

doubly

doubt [doubting doubted]

doubtful doubtless

dough *[bread] doe *[deer]

dove dovecote

dow do

dowdy dowdier

down [downing downed]

downstairs downstream

downwards downwind

downy

dowtful doubtful

doze dozy dozier

[dozing dozed]

dozen

drag [dragging dragged]

draggen dragon

dragon dragonfly

drain [draining drained]

drainage drainpipe

drake

drama dramatic

dramatically

dramatise

[dramatising dramatised]

drank

drastic drastically

draught draughty

draw *[pull, art]

[drawing drew]

drawer *[box]

drawn drawn-out

dread [dreading dreaded]

dreadful dreadfully

dream [dreaming dreamt]

dreamy dreamier

dreary drearier

dred dread

dredge [dredging dredged]

dreem dream

dregs

drej dredge

dreme dream

drench [drenching drenched]

dresarje dressage

dress [dressing dressed]

dress dresses dressmaker

dressage

drew

drey
dribble [dribbling dribbled]
dribiling — dribbling
dride — dried
drie — dry
dried
drier *[less wet] dryer *[machine]
drift [drifting drifted]
drill [drilling drilled]
drink [drinking drank drunk]
drip [dripping dripped]
drive [driving drove driven]
drizzle [drizzling drizzled]
drone [droning droned]
drool [drooling drooled]
droop *[down] droopy
[drooping drooped]
drop *[let fall]
drore — draw *[pull, art]
drawer *[box]
drought
drove
drown [drowning drowned]
drowsy drowsier
drowt — drought
drudge drudgery
drue — drew
drug [drugging drugged]
drule — drool
drum [drumming drummed]
drunk drunkenly
dry [dries drying dried]
dryer *[machine] drier *[less wet]
dryve — drive
du — dew *[drops]
do *[get done]
due *[owing]
dual *[two] duel *[fight]
jewel *[gem]
dub [dubbing dubbed]
dubbul — double
duchess duchesses
duck [ducking ducked]
duckling
dud
due *[owed] dew *[drops]
do *[get done]
Jew *[religion]
duel *[fight] dual *[two]
duet
duffel coat
duke
dull duller dullness
dum — dumb
dumb dumber dumbest
dummy dummies

dump [dumping dumped]
dumpling
dumpy dumpier
dune
dung
dungarees
dungeon
dunjon dungeon
duo
Dupiter Jupiter
duplicate duplication
[duplicating duplicated]
during
durt dirt
dury jury
dusk dusky duskier
dust [dusting dusted]
dusty dustier
dutiful dutifully
duty duties
duv dove
duvay duvet
duvet
duwel dual *[two]
duel *[fight]

duz does
duzn't doesn't
duzzen dozen
dwarf dwarves
dwell [dwelling dwelled dwelt]
dworf dwarf

dye *[colour] die *[death]
dyeing *[colour]
dying *[death]
dylute dilute
dynamic
dynamite
dynamo
dynasty
dynosaur dinosaur
Dyoon June
dysabul disable
dysentery
dyslexia dyslexic
dyspraxia dyspraxic

each

eager eagerly eagerness

eagle eaglet

ear ~ache ~phones ~plugs

ear ~ring ~shot ~wig

eares ears

early earlier earliest

earn *[money] urn *[vase]

[earning earned]

earnings

earth earthly

earthquake

earthworm

eary eerie *[scary]

eyrie *[nest]

east ~erly ~ern ~wards

Easter

easy easier easiest easily

eat [eating ate eaten]

ebb [ebbing ebbed]

eccentric

ech each

echo [echoes echoing echoed]

ecksact exact

ecksamin examine

ecksaminashun examination

ecksampul example

ecksceed exceed

eckscite excite

eclipse

ecology ecologist

ecsentric eccentric

eczema

edebul edible

edge [edging edged]

edgy edgier edgiest

edible

edition *[copy] addition *[sum]

edj edge

educashun education

education

eel

eer ear

eerie *[scary] eyrie *[nest]

eerily eeriness

eese ease

eest east

Eester Easter

eestern eastern

eesy easy

eet eat

eeves eaves

eezee easy

efect   effect *[result]
    affect *[alter]
effect *[result]   affect *[alter]
effective   effectively
effectiveness
efficiency
efficient   efficiently
effort
effortless   effortlessly
efishent   efficient
efishuncy   efficiency
efort   effort
eg   egg
ege   edge
egect   eject
eger   eager
egg [egging egged]
egg   ~cup ~shell
Egipshuns   Egyptians
egsact   exact

egsaggerate   exaggerate
egsample   example
egul   eagle
Egyptians
egzotic   exotic

Eiffel Tower
eight *[number]   ate *[food]
eighteen   eighteenth
eighth
eighty   eighties   eightieth
eigt   eight
eigth   eighth
either
eject [ejecting ejected]
eji   edgy
ekcentrik   eccentric

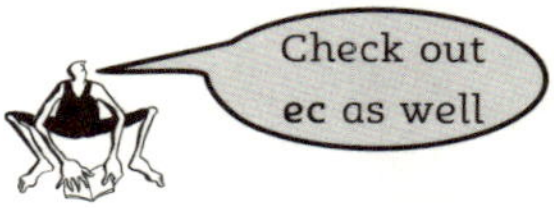

eko   echo
eksampul   example
eksentric   eccentric
eksma   eczema
ekwivalent   equivalent
elament   element
elastic   elasticity
Elastoplast™
elavatid   elevated
elbow [elbowing elbowed]
elder   elderly   eldest
elderberry   elderberries
eldur   elder
election

electric electrical
electrically
electricity electrician
electricle electrical
electrify [electrifies]
[electrifying electrified]
electrocute [electrocuted]
electrocution
electron
electronic electronically
eleet elite
elefant elephant
elekshun election
elektrik electric
elektrisitee electricity
element
elevate [elevated] elevator
eleven eleventh
elf elves elfin elfish
eligible
eliminate [eliminating eliminated]
Elisabethun Elizabethan
eliterashun alliteration
Elizabethan
elk
elm
eloap elope
elongated

elope [eloping eloped]
else ~where
elude [eluding eluded]
elushun illusion *[fantasy]
allusion *[hint]
email
emarald emerald
embalm [embalmed]
embankment
embarass embarrass
embark [embarking embarked]
embarm embalm
embarrass embarrassment
[embarrassing embarrassed]
embassy embassies
embers
emblem
embrace [embracing embraced]
embrio embryo
embroider [embroidered]
embroidery
embroyder embroider
embryo
emerald
emerge [emerging emerged]
emergency emergencies
emfasis emphasis

emigrant *[exits] immigrant *[arrives]
emigrate *[exit] immigrate *[arrive]
[emigrating emigrated]
emigration *[exit] immigration *[arrival]
emoshun emotion
emotion
emotional emotionally
emperor empress
empire *[lands] umpire *[game]
employ [employing employed]
employee employer
employment
emprer emperor
empty emptier emptiest
emrald emerald
emtee empty
emu
emurge emerge
enabel enable
enable [enabling enabled]
enamel
encampment
enchant enchantment
[enchanting enchanted]
enchantress

enciclopeedia encyclopaedia
enclose [enclosing enclosed]
enclosure
encoar encore
encore
encounter
[encountering encountered]
encourage encouragement
[encouraging encouraged]
encownter encounter
encyclopaedia encyclopaedic
end [ending ended]
endanger
[endangering endangered]
endeavour
[endeavouring endeavoured]
endever endeavour
endid ended
endless endlessly
endurance
endure [enduring endured]
enemy enemies
energetic energetically
energy energies
enerjy energy
enething anything
enforce [enforcing enforced]
enforse enforce

engage [engaging engaged]
engagement
Engerlish English
engine
engineer engineering
English
engrave [engraving engraved]
engraver
engrossed
engulf [engulfing engulfed]
enjine engine
enjineer engineer
enjoy [enjoying enjoyed]
enjoyable enjoyably
enjoyment
enjure endure
enkurage encourage
enlarge [enlarging enlarged]
enlargement
enlist [enlisting enlisted]
enmie enemy
enormous enormously
enough
enquire enquiry
enrage [enraged]
enrol [enrolling enrolled]
ensime enzyme
ensure [ensuring ensured]
ensyclopeedia encyclopaedia
entangle [entangled]
enter [entering entered]
enterprise enterprising
entertain entertainment
[entertaining entertained]
enthoosiasum enthusiasm
enthusiasm enthusiast
enthusiastic enthusiastically
entire entirely
entrance entrant
entrust [entrusting entrusted]
entry entries
entur enter
enturtain entertain
entyre entire
enuff enough
enurjetic energetic
envee envy
envelop *[surround]*
[enveloping enveloped]
envelope *[paper]*
envie envy
envious enviously
enviroment environment
environment
environmental
environmentally

envlope envelope

envy [envies envying envied]

envyronment environment

eny any

enzyme

epic

epidemic

epilepsy epileptic

episewd episode

episode

epitaph

epitarf epitaph

eqewstrian equestrian

equal equally [equalling equalled]

equalise equaliser [equalising equalised]

equality equalities

equation

equator equatorial

equestrian

equilateral

equilibrium

equinox

equip equipment [equipping equipped]

equivalent equivalence

eqwpment equipment

erase [erasing erased]

eratic erratic

erer error

erly early

ernest earnest

erode [eroding eroded]

erosion

errand

erratic erratically

error

erth earth

erupt [erupting erupted]

eruption

esay essay

escalator

escape [escaping escaped]

eschuary estuary

escort [escorting escorted]

esculator escalator

esenshul essential

eskape escape

Eskimo

eskort escort

especially

espinarj espionage

espionage

essay

essential essentially

establish establishment
[establishing established]
estate
estchury estuary
esteem [esteemed]
estern eastern
estimate estimation
[estimating estimated]
estuary estuaries
esy easy
eternal eternally
eternity
ethnic
ethur either
eturnity eternity
euphemism
euro
European
Eurostar™
euthanasia
evacuate evacuation evacuee
[evacuating evacuated]
evade [evading evaded]
evaluate evaluation
[evaluating evaluated]
evaporate evaporation
[evaporating evaporated]
evasive

even evenly evenness
evenchualy eventually
evening
event eventful
eventual eventually
ever ~green ~lasting ~more
every ~body ~day ~one
every ~thing ~where
evict [evicting evicted]
eviction
evidence
evident evidently
evikt evict
evil evilly
evning evening
evolution
evolve [evolving evolved]
evon even
evrewere everywhere
evry every
evur ever
ewe *[sheep] you *[person]
yew *[tree]
exact exactly exactness
exaggerate exaggeration
[exaggerating exaggerated]
exale exhale
exam examination

examine [examining examined]
example
exasperate exasperation
[exasperating exasperated]
excavate excavator
[excavating excavated]
excavation
exceed [exceeding exceeded]
exceedingly
excel [excelling excelled]
excellence excellent
excepshun exception
except [but] accept [take]
exception
exceptional exceptionally
excercise exercise
excershun excursion
excess excessively
exchange [exchanging exchanged]
excitable excitability
excite *[thrill] exit *[out]
excite excitement
excited *[thrilled] exited *[left]
excitedly
exclaim [exclaiming exclaimed]
exclamation
exclude exclusion
[excluding excluded]

exclusive exclusively
excrement
excrete excretion
[excreting excreted]
excursion
excuse [excusing excused]
excusable
excwiset exquisite
execute [executing executed]
execution executioner
executive
exekushun execution
exekute execute
exellent excellent
exempt exemption
exercise [exercising exercised]
exert [exerting exerted]
exertion
exhale [exhaling exhaled]
exhaust exhaustion
[exhausting exhausted]
exhibit exhibitor
[exhibiting exhibited]
exhibition
exhorst exhaust
exibishun exhibition
exibit exhibit
exile [exiling exiled]

exist [existing existed]
existence existent
exit *[out] excite *[thrill]
exitement excitement
exklude exclude
exklusiv exclusive
exkrement excrement
exkurshun excursion
exkuse excuse
exkwisit exquisite
exorcise [exorcising exorcised]
exorcist exorcism
exotic
expand expansion
[expanding expanded]
expanse
expect expectation
[expecting expected]
expectant expectantly
expectayshun expectation
expedishun expedition
expedition
expel [expelling expelled]
expence expense
expense expensive
experense experience
experience
[experiencing experienced]

experiment experimentation
[experimenting experimented]
experimental experimentally
expert expertly
expertees expertise
expertise
expire [expiring expired]
expiry
explain [explaining explained]
explanation explanatory
exploar explore
explode [exploding exploded]
exploit exploitation
[exploiting exploited]
exploration exploratory
explore [exploring explored]
exploshun explosion
explosion explosive
exployt exploit
export [exporting exported]
express [expressing expressed]
expression expressionless
expressive expressively
expulsion
expurt expert
exquisite exquisitely
exseed exceed
exsel excel

exsellense excellence
exsept except
exsert exert
exsite excite
extend [extending extended]
extension
extensive extensively
extent
extention extension
exterior
exterminate exterminator
[exterminating exterminated]
extermination
external externally
extinct extinction
extinguish [extinguishes]
[extinguishing extinguished]
extra ~terrestrial
extract [extracting extracted]

extraordinarily
extraordinary
extravagance extravagant
extravagantly
extream extreme
extreme extremely
extrordinary extraordinary
extrovert
exturminate exterminate
exturnal external
exurcise exercise
exurt exert
eye ~brow ~lash
eye ~lid ~liner
eye ~sight ~witness
Eyemax Imax™
eyether either
eyrie **[nest]* eerie **[scary]*

fable
fabric
fabulous
face *[head]
face *[look] [facing faced]
fachen — fashion
fact factual
facter — factor
factor
factory factories
facts *[true] — fax *[paper]
fad
fade [fading faded]
Fahrenheit
faik — fake
fail [failing failed]
failure
faint [fainting fainted]
faintly
fair *[event] — fare *[bus]
fair *[just]
fair fairly fairness
fair-haired
fairground
fairo — Pharoah
fairy *[sprite] fairies
ferry *[boat]
fairy-godmother
fairytale
faite — fate
faith faithful faithfully
fake [faking faked]
fakt — fact
faktoree — factory
falcon falconry
fale — fail
fall [falling fell fallen]
false falsely falseness
famas — famous
fame famed
familiar familiarity
family families
famine
famished
famous famously
fan [fanning fanned]
fanatic
fancy [fancies]
fancy fancier fanciest
fanfare
fang
fansy — fancy
fantasise [fantasising fantasised]
fantastic fantastically
fantasy fantasies
fantisize — fantasise

fantisy — fantasy
fantom — phantom
far *[distant] — fare *[bus]
faraoh — Pharaoh
faraway
farce
fare *[bus] — fair *[event]
farewell
Far East [the]
Farenheight — Fahrenheit
far-fetched
Farisee — Pharisee
farm ~land ~yard
farsen — fasten
farst — fast
fart [farting farted]
farther *[distant] father *[dad]
farthest
fary — fairy
fascinate fascination
[fascinating fascinated]
fase — face
fashion fashionable
fashionably
fassinate — fascinate
fast [fasting fasted]
fasten [fastening fastened]
fast-forward

fat fatter fattest
fatal fatally
fatality fatalities
fate *[destiny] fête *[festival]
fateful fatefully
faten — fatten
father *[dad] farther *[distant]
Father Christmas
fatherhood
father-in-law
fatherly
fatten [fattening fattened]
fatty fattier fattiest
fault faulty faultless
faun *[myths] fawn *[deer]
fauna
favirite — favourite
favour favourable
favourably
favourite favouritism
favret — favourite
fawlt — fault
fawn *[colour, deer]
fax *[paper] facts *[true]
[faxing faxed]
fayr — fair *[just, event]
fare *[bus]
fayth — faith

faze *[bother] phase *[stage]
[fazed]

fead feed

feal feel

feald field

fear [fearing feared]

fearful fearfully

fearless fearlessly

feasant pheasant

feast [feasting feasted]

feat *[action] feet *[toes]

feather feathered feathery

featherweight

feature [featuring featured]

Febrary February

February

Febuery February

fech fetch

fed

feeblely feebly

feechure featur

feed [feeding fed]

feel [feeling felt]

feeld field

feeler

feend fiend

feer fear

feerse fierce

feest feast

feet *[toes] feat *[action]

feetus foetus

feild field

feind fiend

feirce fierce

fell

fellow

felt felt-tip

female

femenin feminine

feminine

feminist feminism

fence [fencing fenced]

fend [fending fended]

ferm firm

ferment [fermenting fermented]

fern

fernish furnish

ferniture furniture

ferocious ferociously

feroshus ferocious

ferret [ferreting ferreted]

Ferris wheel

ferry ferries

ferst first

ferther further

ferthest furthest

fertile

fertilise fertilisation [fertilising fertilised]

fertility

festival

festive festivities

fetch [fetching fetched]

fête *[festival] fate *[destiny]

fether feather

feud [feuding feuded]

feudal feudalism

fever

feverish feverishly

few *[not many] phew *[exclamation]

fewgitiv fugitive

fewl fuel

fewneral funeral

fewse fuse

fezant pheasant

fial file

fiancé *[man]

fiancée *[lady]

fianl final

fiansay fiancé *[man] fiancée *[lady]

fiar fire

fib [fibbing fibbed]

fibre fibreglass

fibur fibre

ficks fix

fickst fixed

ficshun fiction

fiction fictional

fiddle [fiddling fiddled]

fiddly fiddliest

fidget fidgety [fidgeting fidgeted]

field [fielding fielded]

field ~mouse ~work

fiend fiendish fiendishly

fier fear *[afraid] fire *[flame]

fierce fiercer fiercest

fiercely fierceness

fierse fierce

fiery fierier fieriest

fif five

fiftee fifty

fifteen fifteenth

fifth

fifty fifties fiftieth

fig

figer figure

figerativ figurative

figet fidget

fight [fighting fought]

figurative
figure [figuring figured]
fiksed fixed
fikshun fiction
file [filing filed]
fill [filling filled]
fillet
filly fillies
film [filming filmed]
filosofer philosopher
filth filthier filthiest
filthy
fimail female
fin *[fish] Finn *[person]
final *[last] finally
finale *[last event]
finalist
finarlay finale
finck think
find [finding found]
finder
fine [fining fined]
finely
finerly finally
finger [fingering fingered]
finger ~nail ~print
finish [finishing finished]
finly finally

Finn *[person] fin *[fish]
finsh finish *[end]
fiord
fir *[tree] fur *[coat]
fire [firing fired]
fire ~arm ~brigade
fire extinguisher
fire ~place ~work
firm firmer firmest
firmly
firn fern
firry furry
first firstly
firsty thirsty
firther further
firtile fertile
firy fiery
fish [fishing fished]
fisher fisherman
fishy
fisical physical
fisics physics
fist
fit *[clothes] fight *[hit]
[fitting fitted]
fit *[strong] fitness
fite fight
fiv five

five
fix [fixes fixing fixed]
fixture
fizz [fizzes fizzing fizzed]
fizzle [fizzling fizzled]
fizzy fizzier fizziest
fjord
flabby flabbier flabbiest
flag [flagging flagged]
flake [flaking flaked]
flame [flaming flamed]
flamingo
flan
flannel
flap [flapping flapped]
flare [flaring flared]
flash [flashes flashing flashed]
flash ~back ~light
flashy flashier flashiest
flask
flat flatter flattest flatly
flatten [flattening flattened]
flatter flattery
[flattering flattered]
flaunt [flaunting flaunted]
flaver — flavour
flavour [flavouring flavoured]
flaw *[fault] — floor *[base]
flawed flawless
flea *[insect] — flee *[run]
flecks *[dots] — flex *[bend]
flecksibul — flexible
fledgling
flee *[run] — flea *[insect]
[fleeing fled]
fleece [fleecing fleeced]
fleet
flert — flirt
flesh fleshy
flew *[flight] — flu *[ill]
flewid — fluid
flex *[bend] — flecks *[dots]
[flexes flexing flexed]
flexible flexibility
flick [flicking flicked]
flicker [flickering flickered]
flick-knife flick-knives
flies
flight *[trip] — flit *[dash]
fliing — flying
flimsy flimsier flimsiest
flinch [flinches flinching flinched]
fling [flinging flung]
flint flinty
flip [flipping flipped]
flippant flippantly

flipper
flirt [flirting flirted]
flisse fleece
flit *[dash] flight *[trip]
float [floating floated]
flock [flocking flocked]
floe *[ice] flow *[river]
flog [flogging flogged]
flood [flooding flooded]
floor *[base] flaw *[fault]
floot flute
flop [flopping flopped]
floppy floppier floppiest
floral florist
flornt flaunt
floss
flote float
flour *[food] flower *[bud]
flourish [flourishes]
[flourishing flourished]
flow *[river] floe *[ice]
[flowing flowed]
flower *[plant] flour *[food]
[flowering flowered]
flown
flox flocks
flu *[ill] flew *[fly]
flud flood

fluent fluently
fluff
fluffy fluffier fluffiest
fluid
fluke
flume
flung
fluorescent light
flurish flourish
flush [flushing flushed]
flustered
flute
flutter [fluttering fluttered]
fly *[insect, travel] flies
fly [flies flying flew flown]
foal
foam [foaming foamed]
fobia phobia
focus [focuses focusing focused]
fodder
foe
foetus foetal
fog foggy
foil [foiling foiled]
foke folk
foks fox
fokus focus
fold [folding folded]

fole foal
folk ~lore
foll fall
follow follower
[following followed]
fome foam
fon phone
fond fonder fondest fondly
fone phone
fonic phonic
font
food *[eat] feud *[fight]
fool [fooling fooled]
foolish foolishly
foot ~note ~path ~print
foot ~step ~wear ~work
football footballer
for *[use] fore *[front]
four *[number]
forbid
[forbidding forbade forbidden]
forcast forecast
force [forcing forced]
forceful forcefully
forchoon fortune
ford
fore *[front] for *[use]
four *[number]

fore ~arm ~cast ~ground
fore ~hand ~head ~most
foreboding
foreign foreigner
foren foreign
foresee [foresaw foreseen]
forest forestation
forester forestry
foretell foretold
forever
forfeit
forfit forfeit
forgave
forge [forging forged]
forgery forgeries
forget [forgetting forgot]
forgetful forgetfulness
forgive [forgiving forgave forgiven]
forgiveness
forgot forgotten
forj forge
fork [forking forked]
forlt fault
form [forming formed]
formal
formashun formation
format [formatting formatted]
formation

former formerly
formula formulas formulae
forn faun *[myths]
fawn *[deer]
forna fauna
forrest forest
forse force
fort *[castle] fought *[hit]
thought *[think]
forteen fourteen
forthcoming
fortnight fortnightly
fortunate fortunately
fortune
forty fortieth
forward forwards
fossil fossilise [fossilised]
foster [fostering fostered]
foto photo

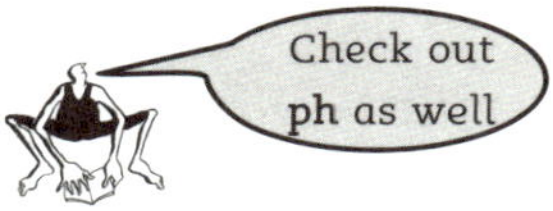

fotograf photograph
fotosynthesis photosynthesis
fought *[hit] fort *[castle]
thought *[think]
foul *[dirty] fowl *[bird]
fouler foulest

found [founding founded]
foundation
fountain
four *[number] for *[use]
fore *[front]

fourbid forbid
fource force
fourhand forehand
fourmula formula
fourt fought *[hit]
fort *[castle]
thought *[think]
fourteen fourteenth
fourth *[4th] forth *[on]
fourtnight fortnight
fowl *[bird] foul *[dirty]
fownd found
fowntain fountain
fox foxes
foyl foil
fraction
fracture [fracturing fractured]
frael frail
fragile
fragment

fragrance   fragrant
fragrense   fragrance
frail   frailer   frailest
frajile   fragile
fraksher   fracture
frakshun   fraction
frale   frail
frame [framing framed]
frank frankly frankness
frankfurter
frankincense
frantic   frantically
frase   phrase
fraud   fraudster
fraught
freak   freakish
freckle   freckled
free [freeing freed]
freedom
freer   freest   freely
freestyle
freeze *[ice]   frieze *[strip]
[freezing froze frozen]
freezer
freind   friend
frekwency   frequency
frekwent   frequent
french

french fries
frend   friend
frens   friends
frenzy   frenzied
frequency   frequencies
frequent   frequently
fresh   fresher   freshest
freshen [freshening freshened]
freshly   freshness
fret *[mope]   threat *[warn]
[fretting fretted]
frew   threw *[ball]
through *[go through]
friar   friary
frickshun   friction
friction
Friday
fridge
fried
friend   ~less ~ship
friendly friendlier friendliest
frieze *[strip]   freeze *[ice]
frigate
frige   fridge
fright *[fear]
frighten [frightening frightened]
frightful   frightfully

frill frilly frilliest
fringe fringed
Frisbee™
frisk [frisking frisked]
frisky friskier friskiest
fritter [frittering frittered]
frivolous
frizzy frizzier frizziest
frog ~man ~spawn
frogmarch [frogmarched]
frolic [frolicked frolicking]
from
frong throng
front
frontier
froot fruit
frord fraud
frorght fraught
frost [frosting frosted]
frostbite frostbitten
frosty frostier frostiest
froth [frothing frothed]
frothy
frown [frowning frowned]
froze frozen
fruit
fruitful fruitfulness
fruitless fruitlessly
fruity fruitier fruitiest
frunt front
fruntier frontier
frustrate frustration
[frustrating frustrated]
frut fruit
fry [frying fried]
fryer frying pan
fryt fright
fucher future
fud food
fude feud
fudge
fue few
fuel [fuelling fuelled]
fugitive
ful fool *[idiot]
full *[complete]
fule fuel
fulfil [fulfilling fulfilled]
full *[up] fool *[idiot]
fullness fully
fumble [fumbling fumbled]
fume [fuming fumed]
fun
function [functioning functioned]
fund [funding funded]
funeral

fungus fungi

funkshun function

funnel

funny funnier funniest

fur *[coat] fir *[tree]

furious furiously

furn fern

furnace

furnish [furnishes]
[furnishing furnished]

furniture

furoshus ferocious

furry *[hairy] fury *[anger]

furrier furriest

furst first

further furthest

furthering

furthermore

furtile fertile

furtilise fertilise

fury *[anger] furry *[hairy]

fuse [fusing fused]

fuss *[worry] fuzz *[fluff]
[fusses fussing fussed]

fussy fussier fussiest

fut foot

future

fuzz

fuzzy fuzzier fuzziest

fyfty fifty

fynd find

fysical physical

fysics physics

fyve five

gabble [gabbling gabbled]
gadget
gael gale
gag [gagging gagged]
gage gauge
gaggle
gaily
gain [gaining gained]
gaip gape
gajet gadget
gala
galaxy galactic
gale gale-force
galery gallery
galleon
gallery galleries
galley
gallon
gallop [galloping galloped]
gallows
galy gaily *[merrily]
galley *[ship]
gamble *[games]
[gambling gambled]
gambol *[frolic]
[gambolling gambolled]
game
gammon

gander
gang ~plank ~way
gangly
gangster
gap *[space] gap-toothed
gape *[look, open] [gaping gaped]
garage
garantey guarantee
garbage
gard guard
garden gardening
gardian guardian
gargle *[throat] [gargling gargled]
gargoyle *[carving]
garige garage
garland
garlic garlicky
garment
garrison
gas
gase gaze
gash gashes
gasp [gasping gasped]
gastly ghastly
gate
gateau gateaux
gatecrash gatecrasher
gather [gathering gathered]

gattoe gateau
gaugius gorgeous
gave
gawky
gayn gain
gayt gate
gaze [gazing gazed]
gear ~box ~stick
geek geeky
geese
gel
gelignite
gelly jelly
gem
Gemini
gender
general
generation
generosity
generous generously
genes *[DNA] jeans *[denim]
genetic
genetic engineering
genetically modified
genie
genius
genral general
gent
gentle gentleness
gentleman
genuine genuinely
geography
geology geologist
geometry
geranium
gerbil
gergle gurgle
geriatric
gerila gorilla
gerl girl
germ
German
germinate germination
[germinating germinated]
gess guess
gest guessed
*[estimated]
guest *[visitor]
gesture
get [getting got]
getto ghetto
gewel jewel

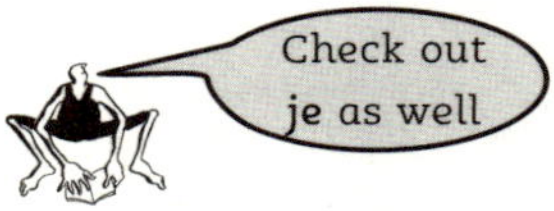

gewelry jewellery

gewish Jewish
geyser
ghastly ghastliest
ghetto ghetto blaster
ghost ghostly
ghoul ghoulish
giant
gibbering gibberish
gidanse guidance
giddy giddiness
gide guide
gier gear
gift
gig *[show] jig *[dance]
gigabyte
gigantic
giggle *[ha ha] jiggle *[jog]
gilotine guillotine
gilt *[gold] guilt *[shame]
giltey guilty
gin
ginee pig guinea pig
ginger gingerly gingery
gingham
giraffe
girgul gurgle
girl girlfriend girlie
giro *[bank] gyro *[spins]

gise guise
gist *[idea] jest *[joke]
gitar guitar
give [giving gave given]
giy guy
Giy Forks Guy Fawkes
glacier glacial
glad gladly gladness
gladiator
glaisha glacier
glamour glamorous
glance [glancing glanced]
gland glandular fever
glare [glaring glared]
glarnse glance
glars glass
glass glasses glassful
glazier
gleam [gleaming gleamed]
glide [gliding glided]
glimmer [glimmering]
glimpse [glimpsed]
glimsped glimpsed
glint
glisten [glistening glistened]
glitter [glittering glittered]
gloat [gloating gloated]
global globally

globe
gloom gloomy
gloomier gloomiest
glossy glossier glossiest
glove
glow glow-worm
glucose
glue [gluing glued]
glutton
gnarled
gnat
gnaw *[bite] nor *[neither]
[gnawing gnawed]
gnome gnomish
go [goes going went]
go go-kart
goal goalie goalkeeper
goat
gob ~smacked ~stopper
gobble [gobbling gobbled]
gobbledegook
goblin
God
god ~dess ~child ~daughter
god ~father ~mother ~parent
god ~send ~son
goggle [goggling goggled]
goggle-eyed

gold ~fish ~mine
golden
golf golf course
gon gone
gone goner
good goodness
goodbye
Good Friday
gooey
gool ghoul
goose goose pimples
gooseberry gooseberries
gorge [gorging gorged]
gorgeous
gorilla
gory goriest
gosling
gospel
gossip
gost ghost
got
goul ghoul
government
gowing going
grab [grabbing grabbed]
grace graceful gracefully
grade
gradual gradually

graf graph
graffiti
graid grade
grail
grain grainy
gram
grammar
grammatically
granade grenade
granchild grandchild
grand ~child ~children
grand ~daughter ~father
grand ~ma ~mother ~pa
grand ~parent ~son ~stand
grandad
granny grannies
graph
grapple [grappling grappled]
gras grass
grase grace *[goodness]*
graze *[feed, cut]*
grasp [grasping grasped]
grass grassy grasshopper
grate *[fire]* great *[big]*
grateful gratefully
grater *[cheese]* greater *[bigger]*
gratest greatest
gratichewd gratitude

gratitude
grave gravely
grave ~digger ~stone ~yard
gravel gravelly
gravity
gravy
gray grey
grayn grain
graze
grdon garden
grease ~paint ~proof
greasy
great *[big]* grate *[fire]*
greater
greatly greatness
greed greedier greediest
greedy greedily
green greenery
green ~grocer ~house
greenhouse
greese grease
greet greetings
greif grief
greive grieve
gremlin
gren green
grenade
grew

grewsome gruesome
grey ~hound
grief grief-stricken
grieve [grieving grieved]
grill [grilling grilled]
grim *[bad]
grime *[dirt]
grimy grimiest
grin [grinning grinned]
grind [grinding ground]
grip [gripping gripped]
grit gritty
grizzly
groan *[moan] grown *[up]
[groaning groaned]
grocer groceries grocery
groggy groggier
grone groan *[moan]
grown *[up]
groom
groop group
groosum gruesome
groove *[slot] grove *[trees]
grope [groping groped]
groser grocer
gross grossly
grotto grottos
grotty grottier grottiest
ground ~less ~sheet ~sman
group
grouse
grove *[wood] groove *[slot]
grovel [grovelling grovelled]
grow growing
growl [growling growled]
grown *[up] groan *[moan]
grownd ground
growth
grub
grubby grubbier grubbiest
grudge grudgingly
grue grew
gruesome
gruff gruffly
gruge grudge
grumble [grumbling grumbled]
grumpy grumpier
grumpiest
grunt [grunting grunted]
grupe group
guarantee guarantees
[guaranteeing guaranteed]
guard guardsman
guardian
gud good
guess [guessing guessed]

guessed *[estimated]
guest *[visitor]
guidance
guide ~book ~lines
[guiding guided]
guillotine
guilt *[shame] gilt *[gold]
guilty guiltier guiltiest
guinea pig
guitar guitarist
gulf Gulf stream
gull
gully gullies
gulp [gulping gulped]
gum ~shield
gun ~boat ~dog ~fight ~fire
gun ~man ~point ~powder
gun ~ship ~shot
gurbil gerbil
gurgle [gurgling gurgled]
gurl girl
guseberry gooseberry
gush [gushes gushing gushed]
gust gusty
gutter guttering
guvern govern
guverment government
guy Guy Fawkes
guzzle [guzzling guzzled]
gym gymnasium
gymkhana
gymnast gymnastics
gypsy gypsies

H-bomb
habit
habitat habitation
hack [hacking hacked]
hackles
hacksaw
had hadn't [had not]
haev have
haf have
hag haggard
haggis
haggle [haggling haggled]
hail [hailing hailed]
hailstone
hair *[head] hare *[animal]
hair ~brush ~cut ~dresser
hairy hairier hairiest
half halves
half ~hour ~way
hall *[room] haul *[pull]
hall ~mark ~way
Halloween
hallucinate hallucination
[hallucinating hallucinated]
halo haloes
halt [halting halted]
halve [halving halved]
ham ~burger

hammer [hammering hammered]
hammock
hamster
hand [handing handed]
hand ~bag ~book ~ful
hand ~made ~shake ~stand
handcuff [handcuffed]
handicap [handicapped]
handkerchief hanky
handle [handling handled]
handsome handsomest
handwriting handwritten
handy handier handiest
handyman
hang [hanging hung]
hangar *[plane]
hanger *[clothes]
hankercheif handkerchief
hankuff handcuff
hanriting handwriting
hanshake handshake
hansome handsome
hapand happened
haphazard haphazardly
hapon happen
hapond happened
happen [happening happened]
happy happier happiest

harbour
hard harder hardest
hard ~board ~ship
harden [hardening hardened]
hardly hardness
hardy hardier hardiest
hare *[animal] hair *[head]
harf half
harm [harming harmed]
harmful harmfully
harmless harmlessly
harmony harmonies
harness harnesses
[harnessing harnessed]
harp harpist
harpoon [harpooned]
harrier jet
harsh harsher harshest
harshly harshness
hartless heartless
harvest [harvesting harvested]
has hasn't [has not]
hassle [hassling hassled]
haste
hasty hastier hastiest
hat *[head] hate *[dislike]
hatch [hatches hatching hatched]
hatchet

hate *[dislike] hat *[head]
[hating hated]
hateful
hath have
hatred
haul *[pull] hall *[room]
[hauling hauled]
haunches
haunt [haunting haunted]
have [has having had]
haven
haven't [have not]
havoc
hawk
hawse hoarse *[voice]
horse *[animal]
hay *[grass] hey *[greet]
hay ~stack ~wire
hayl hail *[ice]
hazard
haze hazy hazier hazily
hazel
he he's [he is, has]
head [heading headed]
headache
head ~dress ~light ~line
head ~master ~mistress
head ~phones ~quarters

heal *[cure]   heel *[foot]
[healing healed]
healer
health   healthy   healthily
healthier   healthiest
heap [heaping heaped]
hear *[sound]   here *[place]
[hearing heard]
heard *[ear]   herd *[animals]
hearse
heart   ~beat ~breaking
heart   ~broken
heartily
heartless   heartlessly
hearty   heartier   heartiest
heat [heating heated] heater
heather
heave [heaving heaved]
heaven   heavenly
heavily   heaviness
heavy   heavier   heaviest
Hebrew
hectare
hectic
he'd [he had, would]
hed   head
hedge [hedging hedged]
hedge   ~hog ~row

heds   heads
heel *[foot]   he'll *[he will]
heer   hear
heffer   heifer
hefty   heftier   heftiest
heifer
height
heighten [heightened]
heir *[inherits]   hair *[head]
heiress   heirloom
heksagon   hexagon
held
helicopter   helipad   heliport
helium
he'll [he will, shall]
hell *[devil]   heel *[foot]
hello *[greet]   halo *[light]
helm   helmsman
helmet
help [helping helped]
helper   helpful   helpfully
helpfulness
helpless   helplessly
helplessness
helter-skelter
helth   health
hemisphere
hen   ~pecked

her *[female] here *[place]

herald [heralding heralded]

herb herbal

herbivore herbivorous

herd *[animals] heard *[ear]

[herding herded]

herdul hurdle

here *[place] hear *[sound]

herl hurl

hermit hermitage

hero heroes

heroic heroically

heroine

heroism

heron

herry hairy

hers *[she owns]

herself

hert hurt

hertul hurtle

hesitant hesitantly

hesitate hesitation

[hesitating hesitated]

heven heaven

hevy heavy

hexagon hexagonal

hey *[greet] hay *[grass]

hi *[greet] high *[tall]

hibernate hibernation

[hibernating hibernated]

hiccup [hiccupping hicupped]

hid *[past of hide]

hide *[not seen] [hiding]

[hid, hidden]

hideous hideously

hidrolik hydraulic

hieght height

hiena hyena

hier hear *[sound]

here *[place]

higher *[taller]

hire *[employ]

hieroglyphics

hiest highest

higeen hygiene

higgledy-piggledy

high *[tall] hi *[greet]

high ~chair ~lands ~lighter

higher *[taller] hire *[employ]

highest highly

highlight [highlighting highlighted]

Highness

hights heights

highway ~man ~men

hijack hijacker

[highjacking highjacked]

hike [hiking hiked]
hilarious
hill ~side
hilly hillier hilliest
hilt
him *[male] hymn *[song]
himself
hind ~quarters ~sight
hinder [hindering hindered]
Hindu Hinduism
hinge [hinging hinged]
hint [hinting hinted]
hip
hiper hyper
hippopotamus
hir her *[female]
hire *[employ]
hirdel hurdle
hire *[employ] higher *[taller]
[hiring hired]
hirl hurl
his *[he owns]
hiss *[sound] hisses
[hissing hissed]
histeria hysteria
histerical hysterical
historian
historic historical

history histories
hit [hitting hit] hitter
hitch [hitches hitching hitched]
hitch-hike hitch-hiker
[hitch-hiking hitch-hiked]
hite height
hiten heighten
hive
hiway highway
hiy high
ho *[shout] hoe *[dig]
hoaks hoax
hoal whole
hoard *[store] horde *[mass]
[hoarding hoarded]
hoarse *[voice] horse *[ride]
hoarsely hoarseness
hoax hoaxes
[hoaxing hoaxed]
hobble [hobbling hobbled]
hobby hobbies
hockey
hoe *[dig] ho *[shout]
[hoeing hoed]
hog [hogging hogged]
Hogmanay
hoist [hoisting hoisted]
hokey hockey

hold [holding held] holder
hole *[gap] whole *[full]
holey *[holes] holy *[sacred]
wholly *[fully]
holiday
holier holiest
hollow [hollowing hollowed]
holly *[tree] holy *[sacred]
wholly *[fully]
Hollywood
holocaust
hologram
holster
holy *[sacred] holly *[tree]
wholly *[fully]
homage
home homely
homeless homelessness
home-made
homesick homesickness
homework
homige homage
homonym
homophone
honer honour
honest honestly honesty
honey ~comb ~moon ~suckle
honk [honking honked]

honour [honouring honoured]
honourable honourably
hood hooded
hoof hooves
hook [hooking hooked]
hooligan hooliganism
hoop *[circle] whoop *[shout]
hoot [hooting hooted]
hooter
hoover™ [hoovering hoovered]
hop *[jump] hope *[wish]
[hopping hopped]
hope [hoping hoped]
hopeful hopefully
hopeless hopelessly
hopital hospital
hopskotch
horde *[mass] hoard *[store]
horer horror
horibul horrible
horid horrid
horific horrific
horizon
horizontal horizontally
hork hawk
horl hall *[room]
haul *[pull]
hormone

horn horned

hornches — haunches

hornet

hornt — haunt

horor — horror

horoscope

horrible horribly

horrid horridly

horrific horrifically

horrify [horrifies]
[horrifying horrified]

horror

horse *[animal] hoarse *[voice]

horse ~fly ~hair ~power

horse ~shoe ~whip

horthorn — hawthorn

hose *[water] hoes *[digs]

hosed

hospital

host [hosting hosted]

hostage

hostel

hostess hostesses

hostile

hostility hostilities

hot hotter hottest hotly

hotel

hot-tempered

houes — house

hound [hounding hounded]

hour *[time] our *[owns]

hourly

hours *[time] ours *[owns]

hourse — hours

house [housing housed]

house ~ful ~hold ~keeper

house ~plant ~proud

house-trained

housewife housework

House of Commons

House of Lords

hovel

hover [hovering hovered]

how *[how much] who *[?]

however

howl [howling howled]

hownd — hound

howse — house

hoyst — hoist

hu — who *[?]

huch — hutch

hud — hood

huddle [huddling huddled]

huff

hug *[clasp] huge *[large]
[hugging hugged]

hugely hugeness

huj huge

huligan hooligan

hulk hulking

hull

hum [humming hummed]

human *[person]

humane *[caring] humanely

humble humbly

humbug

humer humour

humid humidity

humiliate humiliation
[humiliating humiliated]

humility

humorous

humour [humouring humoured]

hump ~back

hunch hunches
[hunching hunched]

hundred hundredth

huney honey

hung

hunger hungrier hungriest

hungry hungrily

hunk

hunny honey

hunt [hunting hunted]

hunter

huntsman

hurbivor herbivore

hurd heard *[sound]
herd *[animals]

hurdle [hurdling hurdled]

huriball horrible

hurikane hurricane

hurl [hurling hurled]

hurmit hermit

hurray

hurricane

hurry hurriedly
[hurries hurrying hurried]

hurse hearse

hurt [hurting hurt]

hurtful

hurtle [hurtling hurtled]

husband

hush [hushed]

husk

husky huskier huskiest

hussel hustle

hustle [hustling hustled]

hut

hutch hutches

huver — hoover™

hy — hi

hybernate — hibernate

hyde — hide

hydraulic

hydrogen

hyena

hyer — higher *[taller]
hire *[employ]

hyest — highest

hygiene hygienist

hygienic

hyjack — hijack

hyke — hike

hymn *[song] — him *[male]

hynd — hind

hyper ~active ~market

hyphen

hypnosis hypnotic

hypnotise [hypnotising hypnotised]

hypnotist hypnotism

hypochondria hypochondriac

hypocrisy hypocrite

hypotenuse

hypothermia

hyre — higher *[taller]
hire *[employ]

hysteria hysterics

hysterical hysterically

hyt — height

hyway — highway

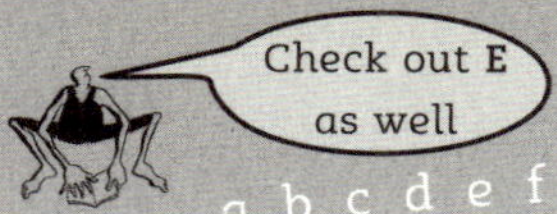

I *[me]   eye *[see]

ice *[cold]   eyes *[see]
[icing iced]

iceberg

icee   icy

ich   itch

icicle

iclispe   eclipse

iconomy   economy

icy icier iciest

icycul   icicle

I'd [I had, would]

idea

ideal ideally

idear   idea

identical identically

identify [identified]

identity identities

idiot idiotic

idle *[lazy]   idol *[worship]

idly

idolise [idolising idolised]

idyllic

idyot   idiot

iether   either *[or]

if

igloo

ignerence   ignorance

ignition

ignor   ignore

ignorance ignorant

ignore [ignoring ignored]

ignorens   ignorance

ignorent   ignorant

iject   eject

iland   island

ilastic   elastic

ile   aisle *[passage]
isle *[island]

I'le   I'll *[I will, shall]

ilegal   illegal

ilegibul   illegible

I'll *[I will, shall]   isle *[island]
aisle *[walk]

ill iller illest

illegal illegally

illegible illegibly

illness

illuminations

illustrate illustrator
[illustrating illustrated]

illustration

ilope   elope

ilustrashun   illustration

I'm [I am]

imaculate   immaculate

image imagery
imaginary [imagining imagined]
imagination imaginative
imagine imaginable
imature immature
imedeate immediate
imens immense
imerse immerse
imige image
imigrate immigrate
imitate imitation imitator
[imitating imitated]
immaculate immaculately
immature immaturity
immediate immediately
immense immensely
immigrant *[in] emigrant *[out]
immigrate *[in] emigrate *[out]
immigration *[in] emigration *[out]
immobile
immoral
immortal immortality
immoshun emotion
immune immunity
immunise [immunised]
imorul immoral
imp impish

impact
impale [impaled]
impashens impatience
impatience
impatient impatiently
impechuous impetuous
impede [impeding impeded]
imperfect imperfectly
impersonate
[impersonating impersonated]
impersonation impersonator
impertinence impertinent
impervious
impetuous impetuously
implament implement
implication
implore [imploring implored]
imply implication
[implying implied]
impolite impoliteness
import [importing imported]
importance
important importantly
impose [imposing imposed]
impossible impossibly
impossibul impossible
impostor
impourtant important

impractical
impresiv impressive
impress [impressing impressed]
impression impressionable
impressionism impressionist
impressive impressively
imprison [imprisoned]
imprisonment
improbable
improper improperly
impropur improper
improve [improving improved]
improvement
improvise improvisation
[improvising improvised]
impruve improve
impulse
impulsive impulsively
impulsiveness
impure
impursonate impersonate
impurtinents impertinence
imunise immunise
in *[go in] inn *[pub]
inability
inaccessible
inaccurate inaccurately
inacsessibul inaccessible

inactive inactivity
inacurate inaccurate
inadequate inadequately
inaksessible inaccessible
inaktivity inactivity
inappropriate inappropriately
inattentive
inbarits embarrassed
in-between
incapable
incense [incensed]
incensitiv insensitive
incentive
incequre insecure
incesant incessant
incessant incessantly
inch inches
inchuitiv intuitive
incident incidentally
incignificant insignificant
incincere insincere
incision
incist insist
incline inclination
[inclining inclined]
include inclusion
[including included]
incoherent

income incoming
incompatible
incompetence
incompetent incompetently
incomplete incompletely
inconceivable inconceivably
inconcistent inconsistent
inconclusive
inconsiderate
inconsiderit inconsiderate
inconsistency inconsistencies
inconsistent inconsistently
inconsolable
inconspicuous
inconspicuously
inconvenient
incorrect incorrectly
increase increasingly
[increasing increased]
incredible incredibly
incubate incubator
[incubating incubated]
incubation
incurable incurably
indecent indecently
indecisive
indeed
indefinite indefinitely

indeks index
independence
independent independently
inderstre industry
indescribable indescribably
indesent indecent
indesisiv indecisive
indestructible
index indices [indexing indexed]
Indian
indicate indication
[indicating indicated]
indicator
indicision indecision
indigestion indigestible
indignant
indigo
indijestion indigestion
indikate indicate
indikayshun indication
indirect indirectly
indiscreet indiscretion
indiscribabul indescribable
indisputable
indistinct indistinctly
indistructabul indestructible
individual individually
individuality

indoor   indoors

indulge   indulgence
[indulging indulged]

indulgent

industree   industry

industrial

industrious   industriously

industry   industries

indyrect   indirect

ineckspensiv   inexpensive

inecksperiens   inexperience

inedible

inefectiv   ineffective

ineffective   ineffectively

inefficiency

inefficient   inefficiently

inekscusabul   inexcusable

inekspensiv   inexpensive

ineksperience   inexperience

inept   ineptly

inequality   inequalities

iner   inner

inescapable   inescapably

inevitability

inevitable   inevitably

inexcusable

inexpensive   inexpensively

inexperience   inexperienced

inexplicable   inexplicably

infachuated   infatuated

infamous   infamously

infancy

infant   infantile

infantry

infatuated   infatuation

infect [infecting infected]

infection

infectious   infectiously

infekshus   infectious

infekt   infect

infent   infant

infentry   infantry

infer [inferring inferred]

inference

inferior   inferiority

inferno

infertile   infertility

infest [infested]

infidel

infidelity   infidelities

infinite   infinitely

infinitee   infinity

infinitive

infinity

infirier   inferior

infirno   inferno

inflamabul inflammable
inflame inflammable
[inflaming inflamed]
inflammation
inflashun inflation
inflate inflatable
[inflating inflated]
inflation
inflaym inflame
inflayt inflate
inflewnce influence
inflexible
inflict [inflicting inflicted]
influence [influencing influenced]
influenshall influential
influential
inform informative
[informing informed]
informal informality
informally
informant
informashun information
information
infrared
infrequent infrequently
infuriate [infuriating infuriated]
ingenious ingeniously
ingenuity
ingrained
ingratitude
ingredient
ingreedyent ingredient
ingury injury
inhabit inhabitant
[inhabiting inhabited]
inhail inhale
inhalation
inhale [inhaling inhaled]
inherit [inherited]
inheritance
inhibit inhibition
[inhibiting inhibited]
inhospitable
inings innings
inishiate initiate
inishul initial
initial initially
initiate initiation
[initiating initiated]
initiative
inject injection
[injecting injected]
injenious ingenious
injer injure
injery injury
injure [injuring injured]

injury injuries
injustice
ink inky
inkling
inklude include

inkrease increase
inkredibul incredible
inkurabul incurable
inkwest inquest
inland
in-laws
inlay inlaid
inlet
inlore in-law
inmate
inn *[pub] in *[go in]
innability inability
innaccurate inaccurate
innedibul inedible
inner innermost
innevitabul inevitable
innings
innocence
innocent innocently
innoculate inoculate
innosent innocent
innovation
innumerable
innundate inundate
inocent innocent
inoculate inoculation
[inoculating inoculated]
inoffensive
inokulate inoculate
inormity enormity
inormous enormous
input [inputting input]
inquest
inquire inquiry
inquisitive inquisitively
inquisitiveness
insane insanely
insanity
inscription
insect
insecure insecurely
insecurity insecurities
insekt insect
insekure insecure
insensitive insensitively
insensitivity
insentiv incentive
inseparable

insert insertion
[inserting inserted]
insessant — incessant
inside
insidens — incidents
insident — incident
insight *[understanding]* — incite *[stir up]*
insignificance
insignificant insignificantly
insincere insincerely
insincerity
insipid insipidness
insishun — incision
insist insistent [insisting insisted]
insistence insistently
insite — incite *[stir up]*, insight *[understanding]*
insolant — insolent
insolence
insolent insolently
insomnia insomniac
insomya — insomnia
inspect inspection inspector
[inspecting inspected]
inspekt — inspect
inspektor — inspector

inspire inspiration
[inspiring inspired]
install [installing installed]
instalment
instance *[example]* — instants *[moments]*
instant instantly
instead
instinct
institushun — institution
institute
institution institutional
instorl — install
instrement — instrument
instruct [instructing instructed]
instruction instructor
instrukt — instruct
instrument instrumental
insufficient insufficiently
insufishent — insufficient
insulate insulation
[insulating insulated]
insulayt — insulate
insulin
insult [insulting insulted]
insurance
insure *[cover]* — ensure *[be sure]*
[insuring insured]

insurt insert
intact
intake
intakt intact
inteereer interior
integrait integrate
integrate integration
[integrating integrated]
integrity
intelecchual intellectual
inteligense intelligence
inteligent intelligent
intellectual intellectually
intelligence
intelligent intelligently
intend [intending intended]
intense intensely
intenshun intention
intenshunal intentional
intensity
intensive intensively
intention intentional
intentionally
interact interaction
[interacting interacted]
interactive
interagayshun interrogation
interest [interesting interested]
interface
interfere interference
[interfering interfered]
interior
interminable interminably
intermission
intermittent intermittently
internal internally
internashunal international
international internationally
Internet
interogate interrogate
interpret interpretation
[interpreting interpreted]
interrogate [interrogated]
interrogation
interrupt interruption
[interrupting interrupted]
intersect intersection
[intersecting intersected]
intersperse [interspersed]
interval
intervene intervention
[intervening intervened]
interview
[interviewing interviewed]
intervue interview
interweave [interwoven]

intestine
intimait intimate
intimate intimately
intimidate intimidation
[intimidating intimidated]
intirier interior
into
intolerable intolerably
intolerance intolerant
intolrabul intolerable
intolrance intolerance
intoxicated intoxication
intreeg intrigue
intrepid intrepidly
intrest interest
intricate intricately
intrigue [intriguing intrigued]
intrikit intricate
introduce
[introducing introduced]
introduction introductory
introjuce introduce
introod intrude
introoshun intrusion
introvert introverted
intrude [intruding intruded]
intrushun intrusion
intrusion intrusive

intuishun intuition
intuition
inturest interest

inturfeer interfere
inturmishun intermission
inturnal internal
Inturnet Internet
inturpret interpret
inturvue interview
intwinded entwined
Inuit
inumerabul innumerable
invade [invading invaded]
invalid
invaluable
invashun invasion
invasion
invayd invade
invent invention inventor
[inventing invented]
inventive inventiveness
invertebrate
invert [inverted]
invest investment investor
[investing invested]

investigate investigation
[investigating investigated]
investigator
invirtibrate invertebrate
invisibility
invisible invisibly
invite invitation
[inviting invited]
involuntary involuntarily
involuntry involuntary
involve [involving involved]
involvement
invurtebrate invertebrate
inward inwardly inwards
inwud inward
iradicate eradicate
irase erase
irate irately
irational irrational

iregular irregular
irelevent irrelevant
ireplaceabul irreplaceable
iresistibul irresistible
iresponsibul irresponsible
ireversibul irreversible

irigate irrigate
Irish
iritabul irritable
iritate irritate
irly early
irn earn *[money]
urn *[vase]
irnest earnest
irning ironing
iron [ironing ironed]
ironic ironically
ironik ironic
ironmongers
irony
irrashunal irrational
irrate irate
irrational irrationally
irregular irregularly
irregularity irregularities
irrelevant irrelevance
irresistible irresistibly
irresponsible irresponsibly
irreverent irreverently
irreversible
irrigate irrigation
[irrigating irrigated]
irritability
irritable irritably

irritate irritation	
[irritating irritated]	
irth	earth
ise	ice *[cold]
	eyes *[see]
ishue	issue
isicul	icicle
ising	icing
Islam Islamic	
island islander	
isle *[island]	aisle *[passage]
isn't [is not]	
isolashun	isolation
isolate [isolating isolated]	
isolation	
isosceles triangle	
isosulees	isosceles
issue [issuing issued]	
isue	issue
it	
italics	

itch [itching itched]	
itchy	
item	
iternal	eternal
iternity	eternity
ither	either
it'll [it will, shall]	
its *[belongs]	it's *[it is, has]
itself	
iturnity	eternity
ivacuate	evacuate
ivaluate	evaluate
ivaporate	evaporate
I've [I have]	
ivolve	evolve
ivory	
ivry	ivory
ivy	
iye	I *[me]
	eye *[see]
iznt	isn't [is not]

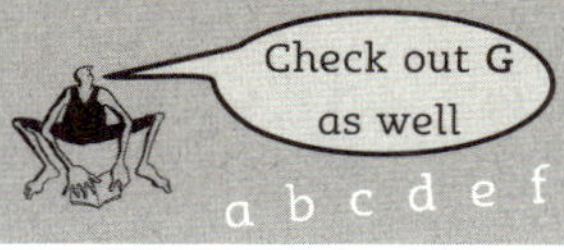

jab [jabbing jabbed]
jack ~daw ~knife ~pot
jackal
jacket
jagged
jaguar
jail [jailing jailed] jailer
jak jack
jaket jacket
jale jail
jam [jamming jammed]
Janery January
jangle [jangling jangled]
January
Janyorary January
jar [jarring jarred]
jargon
javelin
jaw jawbone
jazz jazzy
jealous jealously jealousy

jeans *[denim] genes *[DNA]
jeer [jeering jeered]
jelisy jealousy
jelly jellies jellied
jellyfish
jelus jealous
jentil gentle
jeriatric geriatric
jerk [jerking jerked]
jerky jerkier jerkiest
jernal journal
jerney journey
jersey
jest [jesting jested] jester
Jesus Christ
jet [jetting jetted]
jet-propelled
jetty jetties
Jew *[religion] dew *[drops]
due *[owing]
jewel *[gem] dual *[two]
duel *[fight]
jewelled
jeweller jewellery
Jewish
jewn June
jier jeer
jig [jigging jigged]
jiggle [jiggling jiggled]
jigsaw
jilt [jilted]
jingle [jingling jingled]

jirarf giraffe
jittery
Jluy July
job jobless
jockey jockeys
jodhpurs
jog [jogging jogged]
join [joining joined] joiner
joint jointly
joke [joking joked] joker
jokingly
jolly jollier jolliest
jolt [jolting jolted]
joos deuce *[card]
juice *[drink]
josel jostle
jostle [jostling jostled]
jot [jotting jotted]
journal journalism
journalist
journey
[journeys journeying journeyed]
joust [jousting jousted]
jowst joust
joy joyful joyfully
joyn join
joynt joint
joyride [joyriding]

jubilant
jubilee
judge [judging judged]
judgement
judo
juel duel
jug
juggernaut
juggle [juggling juggled]
juggler
juice *[drink] deuce *[card]
juicy juicier juiciest
jujitsu
July
jumble [jumbling jumbled]
jumbo jet
jump [jumping jumped]
jumper
jumpy jumpier jumpiest
juncshun junction
junction
June *[month] dune *[sand]
jungle jungly
junior
junk
junkshun junction
junyer junior
Jupiter

jurnal	journal
jurney	journey
juror	
jursey	jersey
jury juries	
juse	juice *[drink]
	Jews *[people]
just justly	
justice	

justification	
justify [justifies justifying justified]	
justiss	justice
jut [jutting jutted]	
juvenile	
juwel	jewel *[gem]
Juze	Jews *[people]
	juice *[drink]

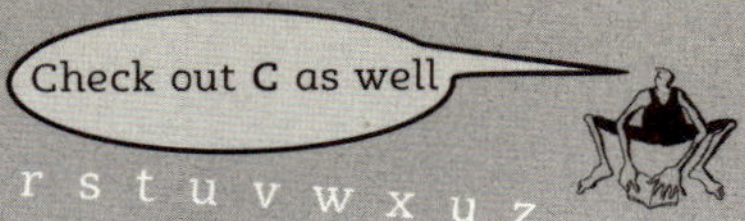

kab	cab
kabbige	cabbage
kafé	café
kage	cage
kaki	khaki
kalculate	calculate
kalculater	calculator
kaleidoscope	
kalender	calendar
kalidoscope	kaleidoscope
kame	came
kamp	camp
kan	can
kangaroo kangaroos	
kanoo	canoe
kapchur	capture
karatee	karate
karaoke	
karate	
kareer	career *[job]
karet	carat *[gold]
	carrot *[veg]
karioke	karaoke
karki	khaki
karnival	carnival
kart [karting]	
kasett	cassette
kaution	caution

kave	cave
kayak [kayaking]	
keal	keel
kean	keen
keap	keep
kebab	
kechup	ketchup
kee	key *[lock]
	quay *[dock]
keel [keeling keeled]	
keen keenly keenness	
keep keeper keepsake [keeping kept]	
keesh	quiche
keg	
kelidoscope	kaleidoscope
kemist	chemist
kennel	
kept	
kerb *[edge]	curb *[stop]
kernel *[seed]	colonel *[army]
kestrel	
ketchup	
kettle kettledrum	
key *[lock]	quay *[dock]
keyboard keyhole keypad	
khaki	
kibab	kebab

kic kick
kichen kitchen
kick [kicking kicked]
kick-off kick-start
kid [kidding kidded]
kidnap kidnapper
[kidnapping kidnapped]
kidney kidneys
kight kite
kik kick
kill [killing killed]
killd killed
killer
kiln
kilo ~byte ~gram
kilo ~metre ~watt
kilt [kilted]
kind kindly kindness
kindergarten
kind-hearted
king kingdom
kingfisher
king-size king-sized
kiosk
kipper
kirb curb *[stop]
kerb *[edge]
kiss [kisses kissing kissed]

kit *[gear] kite *[sky]
kitchen
kite
kitten
kiwi
Kleenex™
kleptomania kleptomaniac
klorafill chlorophyll
knack
knackered
knave *[Jack] nave *[church]
knead *[dough] kneed *[knee]
need *[must have]
knee [knees kneeing kneed]
kneed *[knee] knead *[dough]
need *[have to]
kneel [kneeling knelt]
knew *[fact] new *[not old]
knickers
knick-knack
knife knives
[knifes knifing knifed]
knight *[sir] night *[dark]
knit *[needles] nit *[hair]
night *[dark]
knob knobbly knobblier
knock [knocking knocked]

knock-kneed	
knollage	knowledge
knot *[tie]	not *[no]
knotty	
know *[fact]	no *[not]
know [knowing knew known]	
knowingly	
knowledge knowledgeable	
knowledgeably	
known	
knuckle knuckles [knuckling knuckled]	
koala bear	
kollekshun	collection
Koran	
kore	core *[centre]
	corps *[army]
korgi	corgi
koridor	corridor
korps	corpse
kort	caught *[ball]
	court *[law]
Kouran	Koran

krate	crate
krater	crater
krave	crave
krew	crew
krews	crews *[teams]
	cruise *[trip]
krismus	Christmas

kung fu	
kurb	curb *[stop]
	kerb *[edge]
kurnel	kernel *[seed]
	colonel *[army]
kwack	quack
kwestshun	question
kwestshunaire	questionnaire
kwick	quick
kwiert	quiet

L-plate
labals labels
label
laber labour
laboratory laboratories
laborious laboriously
labour [labouring laboured]
labourer
Labour Party
Labrador
lace [lacing laced] lacy
lack [lacking lacked]
lacquer
lacrosse
lad
ladder
laden
ladle [ladling ladled]
lady ladies
ladybird
laff laugh
lag [lagging lagged]
lager *[beer] larger *[size]
laid
lain *[down] lane *[path]
lair *[den] layer *[cover]
lak lack
lake lakeside
laker lacquer
lakross lacrosse
lamb
lame lamely lameness
lament [lamenting lamented]
lamp lampshade
land [landing landed]
land ~lady ~lord ~mark
land ~mine ~slide
Land Rover™
landscape [landscaping landscaped]
lane *[path] lain *[down]
language
langwij language
lanky lankier lankiest
lantern
lap [lapping lapped]
lapel
lapse [lapsing lapsed]
laptop
larder
larf laugh
large largely largeness
larger *[bigger] lager *[beer]
largest
larj large
lark [larking larked]
larva *[insect] lava *[rock]

larvae
lase lace *[shoes]
laze *[relax]
laser
lash [lashing lashed]
lash lashes
lass lassie lasses
lasso lassos
last [lasting lasted]
lastly
lasue lasso
latch [latches latched]
late lately lateness
latecomer
later *[after] latter *[last]
latest
Latin
latitude
latter *[last] later *[after]
latter latterly
lauf laugh
laugh [laughing laughed]
laughable laughingly
laught laughed
laughter
launch
[launches launching launched]
launder [laundered]
launderette laundry
lava *[rock] larva *[insect]
lavatory lavatories
lavender
law lawyer
lawful lawfully
lawless lawlessness
lawn lawnmower
lay [laying laid]
lay ~about ~man ~out
layer *[cover] lair *[den]
laze *[relax] lace *[shoes]
laze [lazing lazed]
lazer laser
lazy lazier laziest
lead *[metal] led *[took]
lead leaded leaden
lead [leading led]
leader leadership
leaf leaves leafy
leaflet
league
leaisure leisure
leak *[hole] leek *[veg]
[leaking leaked]
leakage
leaky leakier leakiest
lean [leaning leaned leant]

lean leaner leanest	
leant *[past of lean]	lent *[past of lend]
	Lent *[before Easter]
leap [leaping leapt leaped]	
leapfrog	
learn [learning learnt learned]	
lease [leasing leased]	
least	
leather leathery	
leave [leaving left]	
leaves	
leccher	lecture
lectern	
lecture [lecturing lectured]	
lecturn	lectern
led *[guided]	lead *[metal]
leding	leading
ledge	
lee ~ward ~way	
Leebra	Libra
leece	lease
leech leeches	
leed	lead
leef	leaf
leeg	league
leek *[veg]	leak *[hole]
leer [leering leered]	
left left-handed	
leftenant	lieutenant
leftovers	
leg [legging legged]	
legal legally	
legalise [legalising legalised]	
legend legendary	
legibility legibly	
legible	
legislation	
legitimate legitimately	
leisure leisurely	
lej	ledge
lejion	legion
lemon lemonade	
lend [lending lent] lender	
lene	lean
length ~ways ~wise	
lengthen [lengthening lengthened]	
lengthy lengthier lengthiest	
lenient leniently	
lens lenses	
lent *[past of lend]	
Lent *[before Easter]	leant *[past of lean]
lentil	
Leo	

leopard

leotard

lepard — leopard

leper leprosy

lept — leapt

lerch — lurch

lerk — lurk

lern — learn

lesher — leisure

less lesser least

lessen *[reduce] [lessening lessened]

lesson *[class]

let [letting let]

lethal lethally

lethargic

lether — leather

letiss — lettuce

letter lettering

lettuce

leukaemia

level [levelling levelled]

lever

liable

liaise [liaising liaised]

liaison

liar *[lies] — lyre *[music]

liase — liaise

libel

liberal liberally

Liberal Democrat Party

liberate [liberating liberated]

liberty liberties

Libra

libral — liberal

librarian

library libraries

librury — library

lice

licence *[document]

license *[allow] [licensing licensed]

lichen

lick [licking licked]

licker — liquor

lickoriss — liquorice

lid lidded

lide — lied

lie [lies lying lied]

liebraree — library

lier — leer

lieutenant

life lives

life ~belt ~boat ~buoy

life ~less ~like ~line ~long

life ~span ~style ~time

life-threatening

lift [lifting lifted]

light [lighting lit]
light ~house ~weight
light lighter lightest
lighten [lightening lightened]
lightening *[make lighter]*
lightly lightness
lightning *[flash]*
liing lying
like [liking liked]
likeable
likely likeness
liken [likening likened]
likewise
likwid liquid
lilac
lily lilies
limb [limbed]
lime ~light ~stone
limerick
limit [limiting limited]
limitation
limitless
limousine
limozeen limousine
limp [limping limped]
limpet
linch lynch
line [lining lined]

linear
linen
linesman
linger [lingering lingered]
linguist
lining
link [linking linked]
links *[joins]* lynx *[animal]*
linoleum lino
lion lioness lionesses
lip lip-read
lipstick
liquid
liquidise liquidiser
[liquidising liquidised]
liquor
liquorice
lirch lurch
lire liar *[tells lies]*
lyre *[music]*
liric lyric
lisen listen
lisence licence *[document]*
license *[allow]*
lison listen
lisp [lisping lisped]
lissen listen

list
listen [listening listened]
litel little
liten lighten
literacy literate
literal literally
literature
litewait lightweight
litly lightly
litning lightning
litrcy literacy
litre *[measurement]*
litter *[rubbish]* [littering littered]
little littler littlest
littrit literate
live [living lived]
livelihood
lively livelier liveliest
liver
livestock
livid
lizard
llama
load [loading loaded]
loaf *[bread]* loaves
loaf *[laze]* [loafing loafed]
loan *[lend]* lone *[alone]*
[loaning loaned]
loathe [loathing loathed]
loathsome
lob [lobbing lobbed]
lobster
local locally
locality localities
locamotiv locomotive
locate [located] location
loch *[lake]*
Loch Ness Monster
lock *[door, canal]* [locking locked]
locket
locomotion locomotive
loct locked
locust
lodge [lodging lodged]
lodgings
lods loads
loft
loftier loftiest
log [logging logged]
loge lodge
logic logical logically
logo logos
loiter [loitering loitered]
lojic logic
lok loch *[lake]*
lock *[door]*

lokal local
lokalitee locality
lokate locate
lokomoshun locomotion
lokust locust
loll [lolling lolled]
lollipop lolly lollies
lone *[alone] loan *[lend]
lonely lonelier loneliest
loner
long [longing longed]
longer longest
longingly
longitude
look [looking looked]
look ~alike ~out
loom [looming loomed]
loonatic lunatic
loop [looping looped]
loophole
loose *[not tight] lose *[not win]
loose looser loosest
loosely looseness
loosen [loosening loosened]
loot *[goods] lute *[musical]
[looting looted]
lopsided
lord lordly
Lords [the]
loreful lawful
lorless lawless
lornch launch
lorndree laundry
lornmower lawnmower
lorry lorries
lose *[not win] loose *[not tight]
[losing lost]
loshun lotion
loss losses
lost
lot
lotion
lottery lotteries
lotto
lottree lottery
loud louder loudest
loudly loudness
loud ~mouth ~speaker
lounge [lounging lounged]
lousy lousier lousiest
lout loutish
lovable
love [loving loved] lover
love ~sick ~song
lovely lovelier loveliest
loving lovingly

low lower lowest

low ~lands ~ness

lowd loud

lower [lowering lowered]

lowly lowlier lowliest

lownge lounge

lowsy lousy

lowt lout

loyal loyally

loyalty loyalties

loyer lawyer

loyter loiter

lozenge

lrst last

luck lucky luckier luckiest

lucksurius luxurious

lucksury luxury

lucly luckily

ludicrous ludicrously

lug [lugging lugged]

luggage

luggige luggage

lukeemia leukaemia

lukewarm

lull [lulling lulled]

lullaby lullabies

lumber [lumbering lumbered]

lumberjack

lume loom

luminous

lump [lumping lumped]

lumpy lumpier lumpiest

lunacy lunatic

lunar

lunasy lunacy

lunch lunches

lunchtime

luner lunar

lung

lunge [lunging lunged]

lurch [lurches lurching lurched]

lure [luring lured]

lurk [lurking lurked]

lurn learn

luscious

luse loose *[not tight]*

lose *[not win]*

lush lusher lushest

lushus luscious

lusse loose

lussen loosen

lust lustful lustfully

lute *[music]* loot *[goods]*

luvly lovely

luxurious luxuriously

luxury luxuries

ly — lie

lyase — liaise

lybraree — library

lyce — lice

Lycra™

lyer — liar *[tells lies]

lyre *[music]

lying

lynch [lynching lynched]

lyon — lion

lyre *[music] — liar *[lies]

lyrics lyrical

ma'am
macaroni
macaw
Mach March
mach match
machete
machine machinery
machine-gun
machure mature
mack make
mackerel
mackintosh mackintoshes
macor macaw
mad *[crazy] made *[built]
maid *[girl]
mad madder maddest
mad madly madness
madam
madden [maddening maddened]
made *[built] mad *[crazy]
maid *[girl]
maed made
maer mayor
maffs maths
magazine
mager major
magestic majestic
magesty majesty

maggot
magic magical magically
magician
magistrate
magnesium
magnet magnetic
magnificent magificently
magnify
[magnifies magnifying magnified]
magnification
magnifying glass
magots maggots
magpie
mahogany
maid *[girl] made *[built, did]
mail *[post] male *[man]
[mailing mailed]
maim [maiming maimed]
main *[chief] mane *[hair]
mainly
maintain [maintaining maintained]
maintenance
mait mate
maize *[corn] maze *[lost]
majestic majestically
majesty majesties
majic magic
majishun magician

majistrate magistrate
major
majority
mak make
makaroni macaroni
make [making made] maker
make-believe
making
makintosh mackintosh
maksimum maximum
malaria
male *[man] mail *[post]
malicious maliciously
mall *[shops] maul *[hurt]
mallet
malnewtrishun malnutrition
malnutrition
mame maim
mammal
mammoth
man [manning manned]
man ~eater ~kind ~power
manage manageable
[managing managed]
management
manager *[boss] manger *[box]
mandarin
mane *[hair] main *[chief]

maner manner
manewer manure
mange mangy
manged managed
manger *[box] manager *[boss]
mangle [mangled]
mango mangoes
manhandle
[manhandling manhandled]
mania
maniac *[mad person]
manic *[excited]
manicure
manipulate
[manipulating manipulated]
manipulative
maniqure manicure
manly manlier manliest
manliness
manner *[way] manor *[house]
manners
manor *[house] manner *[way]
manshun mansion
mansion
manslaughter
manslorter manslaughter
mantelpiece
manual manually

manufacture [manufactured]
manufacturer
manure
manuscript
many more most
Maori
map [mapping mapped]
marathon
marble
march *[walk] marches
[marching marched]
March *[month]
mare *[horse] mayor *[city]
margarine
margin
marige marriage
marigold
marina *[harbour]
marine *[army, sea]
marjarin margarine
marjin margin
mark [marking marked]
marker
market [marketing marketed]
markey marquee
marksman
marmalade
maroon [marooned]

marquee
marreid married
marriage
marrow
marry [marries marrying married]
Mars Martian
marsh marshy
Marshan Martian
marshine machine
marshmallow
marsipan marzipan
marst mast
martial arts
Martian
martyr martyrdom
marune maroon
marvel [marvelling marvelled]
marvellous marvellously
marys marries
marzipan
masaker massacre
masarge massage
mascara
mascot
masculine
mash [mashes mashing mashed]
mashetee machete
mashine machine

mask *[cover] masque *[ball]
[masking masked]
maskot mascot
maskulin masculine
mass masses
massacre [massacring massacred]
massage [massaging massaged]
massive massively
mast
master [mastering mastered]
master ~mind ~piece
masterful masterfully
mastermind [masterminded]
mat *[rug] mate *[friend]
matt *[dull]
matador
match matches
[matching matched]
match ~box ~less ~maker
mate [mating mated]
matedor matador
material materialistic
maternal maternally
maternity
mathematician
mathematics mathematical
maths
matinée

matiriel material
matrimony
matrix matrices
matron matronly
matt *[dull] mat *[rug]
matter [mattered]
matting
mattress mattresses
mature maturely maturity
[maturing matured]
maturnal maternal
maul *[hurt] mall *[shops]
[mauling mauled]
mauve
maveles marvellous
maximum
may *[perhaps] May *[month]
maybe
mayday *[SOS] May Day
*[1st May]
mayde made *[built]
maid *[girl]
maym maim
mayonnaise
mayor *[city] mare *[horse]
mayoress
mayt mate
maze *[lost] maize *[corn]

me
meadow
meal ~time
mean *[average, imply]
[meaning meant]
mean meaner meanest
mean *[nasty]
meaning ~ful ~fully ~less
meanly meanness
meant
meantime
meanwhile
measles
measurable
measure measurement
[measuring measured]
meat *[flesh] meet *[hello]
meaty meatier meatiest
mecanic mechanic
Mecca
mechanic mechanical
mechanically
mechanism
medal *[award] meddle *[pry]
medallion
medallist
meddle *[pry] medal *[award]
[meddling meddled]

meddow meadow
media
median
medical medically
medication
medicine medicinal
medieval
meditate meditation
[meditating meditated]
Mediterranean
medium
meek meeker meekest
meekly
meet *[hello] meat *[flesh]
[meeting met]
mega ~byte ~phone
megafone megaphone
Meka Mecca
mekanic mechanic
melen melon
melon
melt [melting melted]
member ~ship
Member of Parliament
membrane
memo
memoirs
memorable memorably

memorial
memorise [memorising memorised]
memory memories
men
menace [menacing menaced]
menay many
mend [mending mended]
meniss menace
menshun mention
mental mentally
mentality
mention [mentioning mentioned]
menu menus
meny many
merang meringue
merchant
merciful mercifully
merciless mercilessly
mercury *[metal]
Mercury *[planet]
mercy mercies
merder murder
merge [merging merged]
meringue
merit [meriting merited]
mermaid
mermer murmur
merry merrier merriest
mersiless merciless
mesels measles
mesh [meshes meshed]
meshurabul measurable
meshure measure
mesige message
mess [messing messed]
message messaging
messenger
messtak mistake
messy messier messiest
met
metafor metaphor
metal metallic
metaphor
meteor meteorite
meter *[gas] metre *[length]
method
methodical methodically
methylated spirits meths
metior meteor
metre *[length] meter *[gas]
metric
mew [mewing mewed]
mewchal mutual
mewseum museum
mewsik music
mewsishan musician

mewtinear mutineer
Mey May
miaow [miaowing miaowed]
mice
micro ~chip ~light
micro ~phone ~scope
micro ~scopic ~wave
midday midnight
middle
Middle East
midge
midget
midia media
midian median
midium medium
midst *[middle] mist *[fog]
missed *[let go]
midul middle
midwife midwives
miget midget
might mite *[insect]
*[strength, may]
mighty mightier mightiest
migraine
migrate migration
[migrating migrated]
migt might
mike

mikroskope microscope
mild milder mildest
mildew
mildly mildness
mile mileage milestone
military
milk [milking milked]
milk ~man ~shake
milky milkier milkiest
Milky Way
mill [milling milled] miller
millennium
milligram millilitre
millimetre
million ~aire ~airess
millionth
millipede
mime [miming mimed]
mimic [mimicking mimicked]
mince
mind [minding minded]
mindless mindlessly
mine [mining mined]
mine ~field ~sweeper
miner *[coal] minor *[lesser]
mineral
minet minute
mingle [mingling mingled]

mini ~beast ~bus ~skirt
miniature
minimum
minister
ministry ministries
mink
minnow
minor *[lesser] miner *[coal]
minority
minstrel
mint
minus
minut minute
minute *[time]
minute *[small] minutely
miracle
miraculous miraculously
mirage
mirarj mirage
mirge merge
mirmade mermaid
mirmer murmur
mirror
misbehave misbehaviour
[misbehaving misbehaved]
miscarriage
miscellaneous
mischief mischievous

mise mice
miser miserly
miserable miserably
misery miseries
misfire [misfiring misfired]
misfit
misfortune
misgide misguide
misgivings
misheard
mishun mission
misjudge [misjudging misjudged]
mislay [mislaying mislaid]
mislead [misleading misled]
misplace [misplaced]
misprint
misrabull miserable
miss [missing missed]
missed *[failed] mist *[fog]
missile
missing
mission
missionary missionaries
misspell [misspelling misspelt]
mist *[fog] missed *[failed]
mistake
[mistaking mistook mistaken]
misterius mysterious

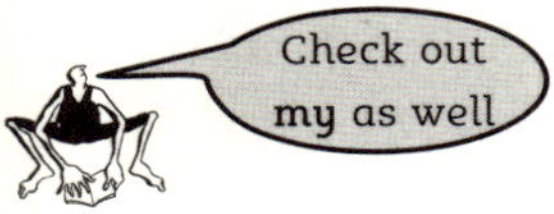

mistic mystic
mistifyed mystified
mistletoe
mistook
mistreat mistreatment
[mistreating mistreated]
mistress mistresses
mistrust [mistrusted]
mistry mystery
misty mistier mistiest
misunderstand
[misunderstanding misunderstood]
misuse [misusing misused]
mite *[insect] might *[strength, may]
mith myth
mity mighty
mix [mixing mixed] mixture
miy my
mizer miser
mizeree misery
mizrabul miserable
mnemonic
moan *[groan] mown *[grass]
moat
mob [mobbing mobbed]
mobile phone
mobility
mock [mocking mocked]
mockery
mode
model [modelling modelled]
modem
moderate moderately
modern
modernise modernisation
[modernising modernised]
modest modestly modesty
modurn modern
moist moisture
moisten [moistening moistened]
molar
molde mould
mole molehill
molecule molecular
molte moult
molten
moment momentous
momentum
monaky monarchy
monarch
monarchy monarchies
monastery monastries

monastic
Monday
money [moneyed]
mongoose
mongrel
monie money
monitor [monitoring monitored]
monk
monkey
monologue
monopolise
[monopolising monopolised]
monopoly
monotonous monotony
monotonously
monsieur
monsoon
monster monstrous
monstrosity monstrosities
monsyer monsieur
month monthly
monument monumental
mony money
moo [mooing mooed]
mood *[temper] mooed *[cow]
moody moodier moodiest
moon ~beam ~light
moon ~lit ~shine

moor *[land] more *[greater]
moor *[boat] [mooring moored]
moorhen
moose *[deer] mousse *[pud]
mooslee muesli
moove move
moovee movie
mop *[clean] [mopping mopped]
mope *[do nothing] [moping moped]
moped *[bike]
mopped *[cleaned]
moral *[good] morally
morale *[confidence]
morality
morbid morbidly
more *[greater] moor *[land]
moreover
morgige mortgage
morl maul *[hurt]
mall *[shops]
mornful mournful
morning
Morse code
morsel
mortal mortality
mortally
mortar
mortgage [mortgaged]

mortuary
mosaic
moshun motion
mosk mosque
moskito mosquito
mosque
mosquito mosquitoes
moss mosses mossy
most mostly
motel
moth motheaten
mother motherhood
motherly
motion motionless
motivate motivator
[motivating motivated]
motivation
motive
motor [motoring motored]
motor ~bike ~boat
motor ~cycle ~cyclist
motor ~ist ~way
motorised
motto mottoes
mould [moulding moulded]
mouldy mouldier mouldiest
moult [moulting moulted]
mound

mount [mounting mounted]
mountain mountainous
mountaineer mountaineering
mourn *[sad] morn *[a.m.]
[mourning mourned]
mournful mournfully
mouse mice
mousse *[pud] moose *[deer]
moustache
mousy
mouth mouthful
move [moving moved]
movement
mow [mowing mowed mown]
mower
mown *[grass] moan *[groan]
mownd mound
mowntain mountain
Mowri Maori
mowse mouse
mowth mouth
moyst moist
much
muck [mucking mucked]
mucky muckier muckiest
mud
muddle [muddling muddled]
muddy muddier muddiest

muing mewing
muel mule
muesli
muffin
muffle [muffling muffled]
mug [mugging mugged]
mule
multicoloured
multicultural
multilingual
multi-millionaire
multiple
multiplication
multiply [multiplies]
[multiplying multiplied]
multiracial
multi-storey
mum
mumble [mumbling mumbled]
mummy mummies
mumps
munch [munching munched]
munches
Mundy Monday
mune moon
muney money
mungrel mongrel
munk monk

munkey monkey
munsh munch
muny money
mural
murang meringue
murcy mercy
murder [murdering murdered]
murderer murderess
murderous
murge merge
murky murkier murkiest
murmaid mermaid
murmur [murmuring murmured]
mursee mercy
mursiful merciful
muscle *[body] mussel *[eat]
[muscling muscled]
muscular
museum
mushy
mushroom
music musical musically
musician
musik music
musishan musician
musium museum
musket musketeer
Muslim

mussel *[eat]   muscle *[body]
must   mustn't [must not]
mustard
mustash   moustache
musty   mustier   mustiest
mutant
mute [muted]
mutineer
mutiny   mutinies
mutter [muttering muttered]
muvabul   movable
muve   move
muzzle [muzzling muzzled]

my   myself
myaow   miaow

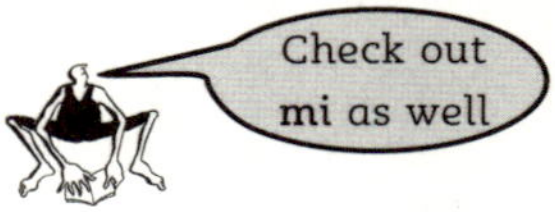

myld   mild
mynah *[bird]   minor *[lesser]
mysterious   mysteriously
mystery   mysteries
mystify [mystifies]
[mystifying mystified]
myth   mythical

nacher   nature
nacheral   natural
nag [nagging nagged]
nail [nailing nailed]
nail-biting
nak   knack
naked   nakedness
nale   nail
name [naming named]
nameless   namely
nanny   nannies
nap [napping napped]
napkin
nappy   nappies
narled   gnarled
narrate   narrator
[narrating narrated]
narration   narrative
narrow   narrower   narrowest
narrowly
narrow-minded
nasal
nash   gnash
nashun   nation
nashunality   nationality
nasty   nastier   nastiest
nat   gnat
nation   nationwide

national
National Health Service
nationality   nationalities
native
Nativity
natural   naturally
naturalist
nature
naughtier   naughtiest
naughty
nausea   nauseous
naval *[navy]   navel *[tummy]
navee   navy
navel *[tummy]   naval *[navy]
navey   navy
navigate   navigator
[navigating navigated]
navigation
navul   naval *[navy]
navel *[tummy]
navy   navies
naw   gnaw *[bite]
nor *[neither]
nawr   now
naybor   neighbour
naytiv   native
nazel   nasal
Nazi   Nazism

nead knead *[dough]
need *[must have]
kneed *[with knee]
neadle needle
near nearer nearest
near nearby nearly
neat neater neatest
neatly neatness
necessarily
necessary
neck necklace
necst next
nectar nectarine
nee knee
need *[must have] knead *[dough]
needle [needling needled]
needless needlessly
needy needier neediest
neel kneel
neer near
neese niece
nefew nephew
negative negatively
neglect neglectful
[neglecting neglected]
negotiate [negotiating negotiated]
neigh [neighing neighed]

neighbour neighbouring
neighbourhood neighbourly
neither
nek neck
nekst next
nelt knelt
nemonic mnemonic
neon
nephew
nerse nurse
nerve nerve-racking
nervous nervously
nervousness nervy
nesessary necessary
nest [nesting nested]
nestle [nestling nestled]
net *[mesh] neat *[tidy]
net netball network
netley neatly
nettle
neuter [neutered]
neutral
never nevertheless
new *[not old] knew *[fact]
newer newest
newly newness
new ~born ~comer
newclear nuclear

newcleus nucleus

newdist nudist

newgar nougat

newmerus numerous

news ~agent ~flash

news ~letter ~paper ~reader

newsons nuisance

newt

newtrishun nutrition

next

nib

nibble [nibbling nibbled]

nice *[kind] niece *[aunt]

nicer nicest nicely

nick [nicking nicked]

nickers knickers

nickname [nicknamed]

niece *[aunt] nice *[kind]

nieghbour neighbour

nier near

niese niece

niet night

nife knife

night *[dark] knight *[man]

night ~club ~dress ~fall

night ~shirt ~time

nightingale

nightly

nightmare nightmarish

nihgt night

nikname nickname

nil

nilon nylon

nimble nimbly

nimf nymph

nine ninth

nineteen nineteenth

ninety nineties ninetieth

ninteen nineteen

nip [nipping nipped]

nipple

nirve nerve

nirvos nervous

nise nice *[kind]

nit *[insect] knit *[wool]

nite knight *[man]
night *[dark]

nither neither

nitrogen

nitting knitting

no *[not] know *[fact]
noble nobleman nobility
nobler noblest nobly
nobody
nock knock
nocturnal
nod [nodding nodded]
noise noiseless noiselessly
noisy noisier noisiest
nollij knowledge
nomad nomadic
nome gnome
noncense nonsense
none *[not any] nun *[God]
non-existent
non-fiction
nonsense
non-starter
non-stop
noodle
noon *[midday]
no one *[not any person]
noose
noospaper newspaper
nor *[neither] gnaw *[bite]
norghty naughty
norm
normal normality

normally
Norman Conquest
normly normally
norsea nausea
norseus nauseous
north ~bound north-east
north ~erly ~ern ~erner
North Pole
north ~wards north-west
norty naughty
nose *[face] knows *[fact]
nosedive [nosedived]
nostril
nosy nosier nosiest
not *[no] knot *[tie]
notch notches
note [noting noted]
note ~book ~card
note ~pad ~paper
nothing nothingness
notice [noticing noticed]
noticeable noticeably
noticeboard
notiss notice
nought
noun *[word] known *[fact]
nourish nourishment
[nourishing nourished]

novel novelist
novelty novelties
November
now nowadays
nowere nowhere
nowhere
nowlege knowledge
nown known *[fact]
noun *[word]
nowon no one
noyse noise
noze knows *[fact]
nose *[face]
nozzle
nuckel knuckle
nuclear nuclear power
nucleus nuclei
nude nudity
nudge [nudging nudged]
nue knew *[fact]
new *[not old]
nues news
nugget
nuisance
nuj nudge
numb numbness

number [numbering numbered]
numeracy
numeral
numerasee numeracy
numerator
numerical
numerous
numonia pneumonia
nun *[God] none *[not any]
nurrish nourish
nurse [nursing nursed]
nursery nurseries
nursing home
nurvous nervous
nurvy nervy
nut nutcracker nutshell
nute newt
nuter neuter
nutrition
nutron neutron
nutty nuttier nuttiest
nuzzle [nuzzling nuzzled]
nxte next
nylon
nymph

oad — ode *[poem]
owed *[money]
oaf oafish
oak
oan — own *[belongs]
oar — or *[alternative]
ore *[mineral]
oarsman
oasis oases
oath
obay — obey
obedient obedience
obediently
obedyans — obedience
obeece — obese
obese obesity
obey [obeying obeyed]
obidyant — obedient
object objector
[objecting objected]
objection objectionable
objective
objekt — object
obligation
oblige [obliging obliged]
oblong
oblyge — oblige
obnoxious

oboe oboist
obow — oboe
obscene obscenely
obscure obscurity
obseen — obscene
observant observation
observe observer
[observing observed]
obsessed obsession
obsessive
obskure — obscure
obsolete
obsqure — obscure
obsqurity — obscurity
obstacle
obstinacy
obstinate obstinately
obstruct obstruction
[obstructing obstructed]
obsurd — absurd
obsurve — observe
obtain obtainable
[obtaining obtained]
obtuse angle
obvious obviously
ocashun — occasion
occasional occasionally
occupation

occupy [occupies] [occupying occupied]

occur [occurring occurred]

ocean

ockur occur

o'clock

octagon octagonal

octave

octiv octave

October

octopus octopuses

ocupashun occupation

ocupie occupy

ocur occur

odd odder oddest

oddity oddities

oddly oddments

ode *[poem] owed *[money]

oder odour

odour odourless

ods odds

of *[part] off *[not on]

ofal awful

of course

ofen often

ofense offence

ofensive offensive

ofer offer

off *[not on] of *[part]

offence

offend [offending offended]

offensive offensively

offer [offering offered]

offhand

office officer

official officially

officious officiously

offside

offten often

ofice office

ofiser officer

ofishall official

ofsyd offside

often

oger ogre

ogre

Ogst August

oh *[surprise] owe *[money]

oil [oiling oiled]

oily oilier oiliest

ointment

okcupashun occupation

okcupyd occupied

okcur occur
o'klock o'clock
oksidise oxidise
oksygen oxygen
oktagon octagon
Oktober October
oktopus octopus
old old-fashioned
Olimpic Olympic
olive
Olympic Games
omelette
omen
ominous ominously
omishun omission
omission
omit [omitting omitted]
omlet omelette
omminus ominous
ommit omit
omnivore omnivorous
on ongoing
once *[one time]* wants *[would like]*
one *[single]* won *[victory]*
one one-way
oner owner
onest honest

onion
online
onlooker
only
onomatopoeia onomatopoeic
onse once
onset
onslort onslaught
onto
onts once
onward onwards
onyun onion
ooze [oozing oozed]
opan open
open [opening opened]
openly opener
opera operatic
operashun operation
operate operator [operating operated]
opinion opinionated
oponent opponent
oposit opposite
opponent
opporchunity opportunity
opportunity opportunities
oppose [opposing opposed]
opposite opposition

oppress [oppresses]
[oppressing oppressed]

oppression   oppressor

opra   opera

opropryet   appropriate

opshun   option

opt [opting opted]

optic   optical

optician

optimism   optimistically

optimist   optimistic

option   optional

optishun   optician

opurate   operate

or *[either]   awe *[wonder]
oar *[boat]
ore *[mineral]

oral *[mouth]   aural *[ear]

orally

orange

orang-utan

orbit [orbiting orbited]

orchard

orchestra   orchestral

orchid

ordeal

order [ordering ordered]

orderly

ordinal number

ordinary   ordinarily

ordnary   ordinary

ordur   order

ore *[mineral]   awe *[wonder]
oar *[boat]
or *[either]

orfan   orphan

organ   organist

organic   organically

organise   organisation
[organising organised]

organism

Orgust   August

oriant   orient

oriental

orienteering

origin

original   originally

originality

originate [originating originated]

orijin   origin

orijinal   original

oringe   orange

orkestra   orchestra

orl   all

ornament   ornamental

ornge   orange

orphan orphanage orphaned

ort ought

orthodontist

ortistic autistic

ortum autumn

oshun ocean

osmosis

Ostralyer Australia

ostrich ostriches

ote oat

othar other

otherwise

otter

ouch

ought *[should]*

oughtn't *[should not]*

oul owl

ounce

our *[owns]* are *[we are]*

hour *[time]*

ourang-outang orang-utan

ours *[owns]* hours *[time]*

ourselves

out ~back ~break

out ~board ~burst ~come

out ~door ~fit ~let ~line

out ~look ~number ~patient

out ~right ~set ~side ~skirts

outdo [outdoes]

[outdoing outdid outdone]

outer space

outrayjus outrageous

outrageous

outspoken

outstanding

outward outwardly

outward-bound

outwards

owa our

oval

ovary ovaries

ovel oval

oven ovenproof

over ~act ~arm ~board

over ~cast ~coat ~come

over ~do ~due ~flow

over ~grown ~hang ~hear

over ~heat ~joyed ~land

over ~lap ~look ~seas

over ~time ~weight

overtake [overtaking]

[overtook overtaken]

overwait overweight

overwelm overwhelm

overwhelm [overwhelming]

[overwhelmed]

ovursee — oversee

ow *[pain]

owe *[money] — oh *[surprise]

[owing owed]

owed *[money] — ode *[poem]

owl owlish

own [owning owned]

owner

ownly — only

owtberst — outburst

owtdoor — outdoor

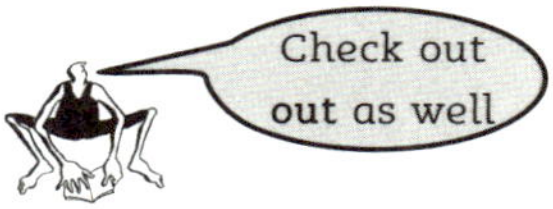

owter — outer

ox oxen oxtail

oxygen

oyel — oil

oyntment — ointment

oyster

ozone layer

pace [pacing paced]
pacemaker
pack [packing packed]
package
packed *[case] pact *[deal]
packet
pact *[deal] packed *[case]
pad *[cloth] paid *[money]
[padding padded]
paddle [paddling paddled]
paddock
pade paid
padlock [padlocked]
pagan
page
paid
pain *[ow!] pane *[glass]
pain ~free ~killer ~less
painful painfully
paint [painting painted]
pair *[two] pare *[trim]
pear *[fruit]
paj page
paket packet
palace palatial
pale *[colour] pail *[bucket]
paler palest
paliss palace

palm palmist
Palm Sunday
pamflet pamphlet
pamper [pampered]
pamphlet
pan pancake
pane *[glass] pain *[ow!]
panel
panic panic-stricken
panicked panicking panicky
panorama panoramic
pansy pansies
pant [panting panted]
panther
pantomime
paper ~back ~work
papier-mâché
parachute [parachuting parachuted]
parade [parading paraded]
paradise
paragraph
parallel parallelogram
paralyse [paralysed]
parashoot parachute
parasite
parcel
parched
pardon [pardoned]

parellel parallel
parent
park [parking parked]
parlement parliament
parliament
parm palm
parrot
parsel parcel
parsley
parsnip
parst past
part [parting parted]
parth path
partly
partner
party parties
pashence patience *[calmness]
patients *[doctor's]
pashent patient
pass [passing passed]
pass passport password
passage passageway
passed *[over] past *[time]
passenger
passige passage
past *[time] passed *[over]

pasta
pastel
pastime
pastry pastries
pat [patting patted]
patch patches [patching patched]
path
pathetic pathetically
patience *[calmness]
patients *[ill people]
patient patiently
patio
patriotic
patrol [patrolling patrolled]
pattern [patterned]
pause *[wait] [pausing paused] paws *[feet]
pave [paving paved]
pavement
paw *[foot] [pawing pawed] poor *[needy]
pore *[skin, scan]
pour *[tip]
pawch porch
paws *[feet] pause *[stop]
pawshun portion
pay [paying paid]
payment
paynt paint

pea
peace *[calm] piece *[part]
peaceful peacefully
peach peaches
peacock
peak *[top] peek *[glance]
[peaking peaked]
peal *[bells] peel *[skin]
peanut
pear *[fruit] pare *[trim]
pearl *[gem] purl *[knit]
pearly
peasant
pebble pebbly
peculiar peculiarity
pedal [pedalling pedalled]
pedestrian
peece peace *[calm]
piece *[part]
peech peach
peek *[glance] peak *[top]
[peeking peeked]
peel *[skin] peal *[bells]
[peeling peeled]
peep [peeping peeped]
peer [peering peered]
peeriodd period
peetza pizza

peg [pegging pegged]
peice peace *[calm]
piece *[part]
pekuliar peculiar
pelican pelican crossing
pelt [pelting pelted]
pen
penalty penalties
pence *[money] pens *[ink]
pencil [pencilled]
penguin
pengwin penguin
penicillin
peninsula
penisillin penicillin
penknife penknives
penniless
pens *[ink] pence *[money]
penshun pension
pensil pencil
pension pensioner
pentagon
pentathlon
people
peple people
pepper peppery
peppermint
pepule people

per cent   percentage
perception   perceptive
perch [perches perching perched]
perchase   purchase
percussion
perfect [perfected]
perfection   perfectly
perform   performance
[performing performed]
perfume
perhaps
perimeter
period
perish [perished]
perm [permed]
permanent   permanently
permission
permit [permitting permitted]
perpendicular
perple   purple
perposs   purpose
perr   purr
perse   purse
persecute [persecuting persecuted]
persenly   personally
persevere   perseverance
[persevering persevered]
persist [persisted]
persistent   persistently
person   personal   personally
personality   personalities
persuade [persuading persuaded]
persuasion
persuasive
persue   pursue
persute   pursuit
perswade   persuade
pesant   peasant
pessimism
pessimist   pessimistic
pest   pesticide
pester [pestering pestered]
pet [petting petted]
petal
petishun   petition
petition
petrify [petrifies]
[petrifying petrified]
petrol
petticoat
pew
pewpil   pupil
phantom
Pharaoh
phase
pheasant

phenomenal phenomenon
phew *[sigh] few *[not many]
philosopher
phoan phone *[telephone]
phobia
phone [phoning phoned]
phonics
photo ~copier
photocopy [photocopied]
photograph [photographed]
photographer photography
photosynthesis
phrase
physical physically
physics
piano pianist
piccher picture
pich pitch
pick [picking picked]
pick ~axe ~pocket
pickle [pickled]
picnic picnickers [picnicking picnicked]
picture [pictured]
pie
piece *[part] peace *[calm]
[piecing pieced]

pieneer pioneer
pierce [piercing pierced]
pierse pierce
pig piglet
pigeon pigeonhole
piggy ~back ~bank
pigheaded
pigsty pigsties
pijarmas pyjamas
pik pick
pikcher picture
pile [piling piled]
pilfer [pilfering pilfered]
pilgrim pilgrimage
pill
pillar pillarbox
pillow pillowcase
pilon pylon
pilot [piloting piloted]
pimple pimply
pin *[point] pine *[tree, sad]
pinch [pinches pinching pinched]
pine [pining pined]
pineapple
ping-pong
pink pinker pinkest
pint
pioneer [pioneering]

pip *[seed]
pipe *[tube] [piping piped]
piramid pyramid
pirate piracy
pirote pirate
Pisces
pistil *[flower]
pistol *[gun]
pitch pitches [pitched]
pithon python
pity [pities pitying pitied]
pixie
pizza
place [placing placed]
plaed played
plague [plaguing plagued]
plain plainly
plait *[hair] plate *[dish]
[plaiting plaited]
plan [planning planned]
plane *[aircraft] plain *[basic]
planet planetary
plank
plant [planting planted]
plasis places
plaster [plastering plastered]
plastic
Plasticine™

plat plait
plate *[dish] plait *[hair]
platform
play [playing played]
play ~ground ~group ~mate
play ~school ~script ~time
playd played
playful playfully
plead [pleading pleaded]
pleasant pleasantly
please [pleasing pleased]
pleasure pleasurable
pleat [pleated]
pledge [pledging pledged]
pleeze please
plenty plentiful
plezant pleasant
plezure pleasure
plight *[state] polite *[good]
plimsolls
plite plight *[state]
polite *[good]
plod [plodding plodded]
plot [plotting plotted]
plough [ploughing ploughed]
plow plough
pluck [plucked]
plucky pluckier pluckiest

plug [plugging plugged]
plum *[fruit] plume *[feather]
plumber plumbing
plummer plumber
plump plumper plumpest
plunder [plundered]
plunge [plunging plunged]
plus
plyte plight
pneumonia
poach poacher
[poaching poached]
poak poke
poar paw *[foot]
poor *[needy]
pore *[skin, scan]
pour *[liquid]
poch poach
pocket pocketful
[pocketing pocketed]
pod
podgy podgier podgiest
poem
poepel people
poet poetic poetical
poetry
pogy podgy
point [pointing pointed]

pointless pointlessly
poise [poised]
poison poisonous
[poisoning poisoned]
poitree poetry
poke [poking poked]
poker
poket pocket
pokey
polar polar bear
pole *[stick] poll *[vote]
pole vault
polees police
poler polar
police ~man ~woman
policy policies
poligon polygon
polish [polishing polished]
poliss police
polite *[good] plight *[state]
politely politeness
politheen polythene
political politician
politics
politishun politician
poll *[vote] pole *[stick]
pollen
pollinate [pollinated]

pollination

pollute [polluting polluted]

pollution

polo

poloot   pollute

poltry   poultry

polygon

polyte   polite

polythene

pome   poem

pompous   pompously

pond

ponder [pondered]

ponee   pony

pony   ponies

ponytail

poodle

pool *[water]   pull *[move]

pool *[collect] [pooling pooled]

poor *[needy]   paw *[foot]
pore *[skin, scan]
pour *[liquid]

poorer   poorest   poorly

pop [popping popped]

popcorn

Pope [the]

poplar *[tree]   popular *[liked]

poppy   poppies

popular   popularity

populated   population

por   paw *[foot]
poor *[needy]
pore *[skin, scan]
pour *[liquid]

porch   porches

porcupine

pore *[skin, scan] [poring pored]   paw *[foot]
poor *[needy]
pour *[liquid]

pork

pornch   paunch

porridge

porse   pause *[stop]
paws *[feet]

porshun   portion

port   portable

porter

portion

portrait

poscher   posture

pose [posing posed]

posession   possession

posh   posher   poshest

poshun   potion

posishun   position

position [positioned]

positive positively
possess
[possesses possessing possessed]
possession
possessive possessively
possibility possibilities
possible possibly
post [posting posted]
post ~box ~card ~code
post ~man ~mark ~office
postage postage stamp
postal postal order
poster
postige postage
post-mortem
postpone [postponing postponed]
posture
posy posies
posytiv positive
pot [potting potted]
pot-belly
pot ~hole ~holing
potato potatoes
potenshul potential
potential potentially
potion
potter [pottering pottered]
pottery potteries

pottry pottery
pouch pouches
poultry
pounce [pouncing pounced]
pound [pounding pounded]
pour *[liquid] paw *[foot]
[pouring poured] poor *[needy]
pore *[skin, scan]
pout [pouting pouted]
poverty
powch pouch
powder [powdered] powdery
power [powered] powerless
powerful powerfully
power station
pownd pound
pownse pounce
powt pout
powur power
poynt point
poyson poison
poze pose
practical practically
practice *[way]
practise *[do] [practising practised]
praer prayer
praise [praising praised]
praktikal practical

pram
prance [prancing pranced]
prank
pranse prance
prawn
pray *[to God] prey *[hunt]
[praying prayed]
prayer
prayse praise
preach [preaches]
[preaching preached]
precarious precariously
precaution
precawshun precaution
precious
precipice
precise precisely precision
precocious
precorshun precaution
predator
predict [predicting predicted]
predictable prediction
preech preach
preen [preening preened]
preest priest
prefer [preferring preferred]
preferable preferably
prefix prefixes

pregnant pregnancy
prehistoric
prejudice [prejudiced]
prekoshus precocious
premature prematurely
preoccupied
preparation preparatory
prepare [preparing prepared]
preposition
prescribe [prescribed]
prescription
presence *[company]
presents *[gifts]
presens presence
present presently
[presenting presented]
presentation
preservation preservative
preserve [preserving preserved]
preshure pressure
preshus precious
president presidential
presise precise
press [presses]
[pressing pressed]
pressure pressurised
presume [presumed]
presumably

pretect protect
pretence
pretend [pretending pretended]
pretty prettier prettiest
prevent prevention
[preventing prevented]
previde provide
previous previously
prey *[hunt] pray *[to God]
[preying preyed]
prezant present
price *[cost] prize *[award]
[pricing priced]
priceless
prick [pricking pricked]
prickle [prickling prickled]
prickly
pride *[self-respect] pried *[snooped]
pridict predict

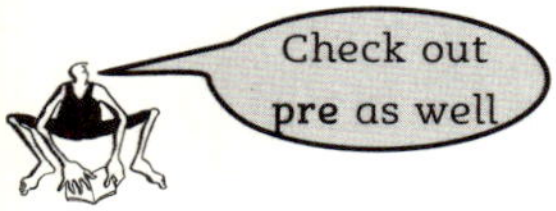

pridikshun prediction
pries *[snoops] prize *[award]
priest priestess
prifer prefer
prihistoric prehistoric
prik prick
prikul prickle
prim primly primness
primary
prime [primed]
prime minister
prime number
primitive
primrose
prince princely princess
principal *[chief]
principle *[rule, idea]
prinse prince
print [printing printed]
priority priorities
pripair prepare
priscribe prescribe
priscripshun prescription
priservativ preservative
prism
prison prisoner
prisume presume
prisurve preserve
pritend pretend
prity pretty
privacy
private privately
privent prevent

privilege [privileged]

privvasee — privacy

prize *[award] — price *[cost]

probable probably

probe [probing probed]

probible — probable

problem

proceed [proceeding proceeded]

process [processes] [processing processed]

procession

proclaim [proclaiming proclaimed]

prod [prodding prodded]

produce [producing produced]

producer

product production

produse — produce

profesee — prophecy

profeshun — profession

profession professional

professor

profet — prophet *[seer] — profit *[gain]

proffesor — professor

profile

profit *[gain] — prophet *[seer]
[profiting profited]

progect — project

program *[computer]
[programming programmed]

programme *[events]

progress [progressing progressed]

project projector

promise [promising promised]

promiss — promise

promoshun — promotion

promote [promoted]

promotion promotional

prompt [prompting prompted]

promptly

promt — prompt

prone

prong

pronoun

pronounce
[pronouncing pronounced]

pronounciation — pronunciation

pronown — pronoun

pronunciation

proof *[fact] — prove *[show]

proon — prune

proov — prove

prop [propping propped]

propel [propelled] propeller

proper properly

property properties

prophecy *[prediction]*

prophesy *[predict]*

[prophesies prophesied]

prophet prophetic

proporshun proportion

proportion

propose proposal

[proposing proposed]

prorn prawn

prose

prosecute [prosecuted]

proseed proceed

prosequte prosecute

prosess process

prospect

protecshun protection

protect protection

[protecting protected]

protective protectively

proteen protein

protein

protest [protesting protested]

proud prouder proudest

proudly

prove *[show]* proof *[fact]*

proverb proverbial

provide [providing provided]

provision provisional

provocative

provoke [provoked]

prow

prowd proud

prowl [prowling prowled]

pruf proof *[fact]*

prove *[show]*

prune [pruning pruned]

pruve prove

pry [pries prying pried]

pryde pride

psychological

psychology psychologist

pterodactyl

pub

puberty

public publicity

publication

publik public

publish publisher

[publishing published]

publisity publicity

puce

pudding

puddle

pudel puddle

puff [puffing puffed]

puffin

pule	pull
pull *[move]	pool *[water]
[pulling pulled]	
pullover	
pulp [pulped]	
pulpit	
pulse	
puma pumas	
pumel	pummel
pumkin	pumpkin
pump [pumping pumped]	
pumpkin	
pun	
puncchual	punctual
punch [punches punching punched]	
punctual punctuality	
punctuate punctuation	
puncture	
punish [punishes]	
[punishing punished]	
punishment	
punkture	puncture
punnet	
puny punier puniest	
pupa pupae	
pupil	
puppet	
puppy puppies	

pur	per *[rate]

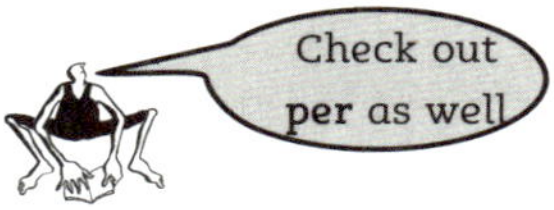

purcentage	percentage
purchase [purchased]	
purcushon	percussion
purd	purred
pure *[perfect]	purr *[cat]
pure purely	
purfict	perfect
purform	perform
purfume	perfume
purhaps	perhaps
purify [purified]	
purm	perm
purmanent	permanent
puroved	proved
purple	
purpose purposely	
purr *[cat]	per *[rate]
[purring purred]	
purrfikt	perfect
purse	
pursecutid	persecuted
pursevure	persevere
pursue [pursuing pursued]	
pursuit	

push [pushes pushing pushed]
put *[place] [putting put]
putt *[golf] [putting putted]
putty
puzzle [puzzling puzzled]
pyjamas
pyle pile

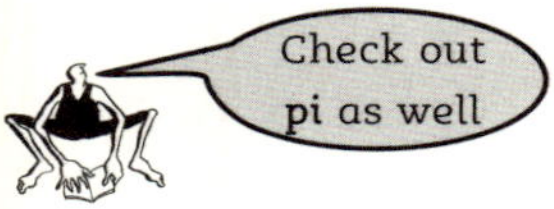

pylon
pynt pint
pyramid
pyrit pirate
Pysees Pisces
python
pyur pure

qake — quake
qarrel — quarrel
qarter — quarter
qeschun — question
quack [quacking quacked]
quadratic equation
quadrilateral
quadruple [quadrupled]
quaint quainter quaintest
quak — quack
quake [quaking quaked]
Quaker
qualification
qualify [qualifies]
[qualifying qualified]
quality qualities
quantity quantities
quarantine
quarrel quarrelsome
[quarrelling quarrelled]
quarry quarries
quart
quarter
quartet
quarts *[measure]*
quartz *[mineral]*
quaree — quarry
quay *[sea]* — key *[lock, main]*
que — cue *[billiards]*
queue *[line up]*
queasy queasier queasiest
queen
queer queerer queerest
queerly
queery — query
queezy — queasy
queiten — quieten
quell [quelling quelled]
quench [quenching quenched]
query queries [querying queried]
quest
question [questioning questioned]
questionable
questionnaire
queue *[line]* — cue *[ball]*
[queueing queued]
quiat — quiet
quibble [quibbling quibbled]
quick quicker quickest
quicken [quickening quickened]
quickly quickness
quicksand
quick-tempered
quick-witted
quicley — quickly
quid

quier queer
quiet *[silent] quite *[rather]
quieten [quietening quietened]
quieter quietest
quietly
quilt [quilted]
quirky quirkier
quit *[leave, stop]
[quitting quitted quit]
quite *[rather] quiet *[silent]
quitter
quiver [quivering quivered]
quiz quizzes [quizzing quizzed]
quodratic quadratic

quolify qualify
quolity quality
quontity quantity
quorrel quarrel
quorry quarry
quorter quarter
quorts quarts *[measure]
quartz *[mineral]
quoruntine quarantine
quota
quotashun quotation
quotation
quote [quoting quoted]
qwack quack
qwench quench
qwick quick
qwit quit
qwod quad
qworter quarter
qwote quote

rabbit
rabeys rabies
rabies rabid
race *[win] raise *[lift]
[racing raced]
racehorse
racial racism racist
rack *[shelf] rake *[leaves]
racket *[din] racquet *[bat]
radar
radiator
radio radios
radioactive radioactivity
radius
radyo radio
raffle [raffling raffled]
raft [rafting rafted]
rag *[cloth] rage *[fury]
rage *[fury] [raging raged]
ragged *[torn] raged *[fury]
raid [raiding raided]
rail railway
rain *[water] reign *[rule]
[raining rained] rein *[horse]
rain ~coat ~drop
rain ~fall ~forest
raindeer reindeer
rainy rainier rainiest

raise *[lift] rays *[light]
[raising raised]
raisin
raje rage
rake
ram
ramble rambler
[rambling rambled]
rampage [rampaged]
ramparts
ramshackled
ran
ranch ranches
rane rain *[water]
reign *[rule]
rein *[horse]
rang
range [ranging ranged]
rank rankings
ransack [ransacking ransacked]
ransom [ransomed]
rant [ranting ranted]
rap *[knock] wrap *[pack]
[rapping rapped]
rapper *[pop] wrapper *[case]
rapid rapidly
rare rarer rarest rarely
rasberry raspberry

rascal
rash rashly rashness
rashio ratio
rashun ration
rasisum racism
raspberry raspberries
rat [ratted]
rate [rating rated]
rather
rattle [rattling rattled]
ratty rattier
ravenous ravenously
ravioli
raw *[uncooked] roar *[lion]
raydar radar
rayl rail
rayn rain *[water]
reign *[rule]
rein *[horse]
rays *[light] raise *[lift]
rayser razor
rayshal racial
razor
reach [reaching reached]
react [reacting reacted]
reaction
read *[book] reed *[plant]
[reading read]

reader
ready readier readiest
real *[actual] reel *[spin]
realise realisation
[realising realised]
realism realist
realistic realistically
reality
really *[truly] rely *[trust]
reap reaper [reaping reaped]
reappear reappearance
[reappearing reappeared]
rear *[horse] rare *[scarce]
[rearing reared]
rearrange [rearranged]
reason [reasoned]
reasonable reasonably
reassure reassurance
[reassuring reassured]
rebal rebel
rebel rebellion
[rebelling rebelled]
rebellious rebelliously
rebild rebuild
rebuild [rebuilding rebuilt]
rebuke [rebuked]
recall [recalling recalled]
recede [receding receded]

receipt
receive   receiver
[receiving received]
recent *[latest]   resent *[grudge]
recently
reception   receptionist
receptive
rech   reach *[get]
retch *[vomit]
wretch *[person]
recipe   recipes
recite   recital [reciting recited]
reckless   recklessly
recklessness
reckon [reckoning reckoned]
reclaim [reclaiming reclaimed]
recline [reclining reclined]
recognise   recognisable
[recognising recognised]
recognition
recoil [recoiling recoiled]
recollect   recollection
[recollecting recollected]
recommend   recommendation
[recommending recommended]
reconcile [reconciled]
reconciliation
reconnect [reconnected]

reconsider
[reconsidering reconsidered]
reconsile   reconcile
reconstruct [reconstructed]
record [recording recorded]
recover   recoverable
[recovering recovered]
recovery   recoveries
recreation   recreational
recruit   recruitment
[recruiting recruited]
rectangle   rectangular
recur [recurring recurred]
recurrence   recurrent
recycle [recycled]
red *[colour]   read *[book]
redden [reddening]
reddy   ready
redial [redialling redialled]
redo [redoing redone]
redouble [redoubled]
reduce   reduction
[reducing reduced]
redundancy   redundant
reduse   reduce
reech   reach
reed *[plant]   read *[book]
reek *[smell]   wreak *[havoc]

reel *[spin] real *[true]
reeson reason
refer [referring referred]
referee [refereeing refereed]
reference [referenced]
refill refillable [refilling refilled]
refine [refined] refinement
reflect reflective
[reflecting reflected]
reflection
reflex reflexes
refrain [refrained]
refresh refreshment
[refreshing refreshed]
refrigerate [refrigerated]
refrigeration refrigerator
refuel [refuelling refuelled]
refuge *[shelter]
refugee *[flee] refugees
refund [refunding refunded]
refuree referee
refuse refusal [refusing refused]
regain [regaining regained]
regard regardless
[regarding regarded]
regatta regattas
regay reggae
regect reject

reggae
regiment regimental
region regional
register registration
[registering registered]
regler regular
regret [regretting regretted]
regretful regretfully
regrettable regrettably
regular regularly regularity
rehearse rehearsal
[rehearsing rehearsed]
reheat [reheating reheated]
reign *[rule] rain *[water]
rein *[horse]
[reigning reigned]
rein *[horse] rain *[water]
reign *[rule]
reindeer
reinforce reinforcement
[reinforcing reinforced]
reject [rejecting rejected]
rejection
rejiment regiment
rejister register
rejoice [rejoicing rejoiced]
rejuce reduce
rejun region

rekollekt recollect
rekommend recommend
rekord record
rekwest request
relate [relating related]
relation relationship
relative relatively
relavent relevant
relax relaxation
[relaxes relaxing relaxed]
relay [relaying relayed]
release [releasing released]
relegate relegation
[relegating relegated]
relent [relenting relented]
relentless relentlessly
relevance relevant
reliable reliably
relief
relieve [relieved]
religion
religious religiously
relijion religion
relly really
reluctance
reluctant reluctantly
rely *[trust] really *[truly]
[relies relying relied]

remain remainder
[remaining remained]
remark remarkable
[remarking remarked]
rember remember
remember
[remembering remembered]
remind reminder
[reminding reminded]
remote remoter
remotely remoteness
remove removal
[removing removed]
rendezvous
renew [renewing renewed]
renewable
repair [repairing repaired]
repay repayment
[repaying repaid]
repayd repaid
repeat [repeating repeated]
repeatedly
repel [repelled] repellent
repent [repenting repented]
repere repair
repete repeat
repetition repetitious
repetitive repetitively

replace replaceable
[replacing replaced]
replacement
replay [replaying replayed]
reply replies [replying replied]
report reportedly reporter
[reporting reported]
represent representation
[representing represented]
representative
reprimand [reprimanded]
reproduce
[reproducing reproduced]
reproduction reproductive
reptile reptilian
repulsive repulsively
reputation
request [requesting requested]
require requirement
[requiring required]
rere rare *[scarce]
rear *[back, horse]
rerite rewrite
rerote rewrote
resalootion resolution
rescue rescuer
[rescuing rescued]

research [researches]
[researching researched]
resseet receipt
reseeve receive
resemble [resembling resembled]
resemblance
resent *[grudge] recent *[latest]
resentful resentment
resepshun reception
reservation
reserve [reserved]
reservoir
residence resident
residenchal residential
residential
resign resignation
[resigning resigned]
resipy recipe
resist [resisting resisted]
resistance resistant
resite recite
reskue rescue
resle wrestle
resolution
resolve [resolving resolved]
resons reasons
resort [resorting resorted]
resource resourceful

respect respectable
[respecting respected]
respectful respectfully
respond [responded]
response responsibility
responsibilities
responsible responsibly
resstront restaurant
rest [resting rested]
restaurant
restful restfully
restless restlessly
restore restoration
[restoring restored]
restrain restraint
[restraining restrained]
restrict restriction
[restricting restricted]
result [resulting resulted]
resurvwa reservoir
resuscitate [resuscitated]
resuscitation
resycle recycle
retain [retaining retained]
retaliate [retaliated]
retch *[vomit] [retching]
wretch *[person]
rethink [rethinking rethought]

retire retirement
[retiring retired]
retort [retorting retorted]
retrace [retracing retraced]
retreat [retreating retreated]
retrieve retrievable
[retrieving retrieved]
retriever
retrospect retrospective
return [returning returned]
reunion
reunite [reuniting reunited]
reveal [revealing revealed]
revenge revengeful
reverse reversible
[reversing reversed]
review [reviewed]
revise [revising revised]
revision
revive [reviving revived]
revolt [revolting revolted]
revolution revolutionary
revolutionise [revolutionised]
revolve [revolving revolved]
revolver
reward [rewarding rewarded]
rewind [rewinding rewound]
rezzavwa reservoir

rfter after
rfternon afternoon
rheumatism
rhino rhinoceros
rhomboid rhombus
rhubarb
rhyme [rhyming rhymed]
rhythm rhythmical
riacshun reaction
riact react
riality reality
rib
ribbon
ribellius rebellious
rice *[food] rise *[up]
riceipt receipt
rich richly richness
Richter Scale [the]
rickety
riclaim reclaim
ricoil recoil
rid riddance
riddle
ride rider [riding rode ridden]
ridge ridged
ridiculous ridiculously
rifle [rifling rifled]
riflect reflect

right *[correct] write *[pen]
right rightly rightful
right-handed
rigid rigidly
rim *[edge] rhyme *[poetry]
rimless rimmed
rimain remain

rimark remark
rimember remember
rimote remote
rimoval removal
rind
ring *[circle] wring *[wet]
ring *[bell] [ringing rang rung]
rink
rinkle wrinkle
rino rhino
rinse [rinsing rinsed]
riot [rioting rioted]
riotous riotously
rip *[tear] ripe *[ready]
[ripping ripped]
ripair repair
ripe ripeness
ripeat repeat

ripen [ripening ripened]
riply — reply
riport — report
ripple [rippling rippled]
ripulsiv — repulsive
riquest — request
riquire — require
rise *[up] — rice *[food]
[rises rising risen]
riserve — reserve
risine — resign
risist — resist
risk [risking risked]
risky riskier riskiest
risolve — resolve
risort — resort
risotto
risource — resource
rispect — respect
rispectabul — respectable
risponsibul — responsible
ritch — rich
rithum — rhythm
ritual
riturn — return
rival rivalry
rivenge — revenge
river riverside

rivet [riveting riveted]
ro — roe *[deer]
row *[boat]
road *[street] — rode *[bike]
rowed *[boat]
roam *[wander] — Rome *[city]
[roaming roamed]
roar *[lion] — raw *[uncooked]
[roaring roared]
roast [roasting roasted]
rob [robbed] robbery
robe [robed]
robin
robot robotic
rock [rocking rocked]
rocket
rocky rockier rockiest
rod *[fishing] — rode *[bike]
road *[street]
rowed *[boat]
rodent
roial — royal
rok — rock
roket — rocket
role *[actor]
roll *[move] [rolling rolled] roller
Roman Roman Catholic
romance

romanse romance

romantic romantically

rombus rhombus

Romen Roman

rondayvoo rendezvous

rong wrong

roobarb rhubarb

roof roofless

rook rookery

room roomful roomy

roomer rumour

roost [roosting roosted]

rooster

root *[plant] route *[way]
[rooting rooted]

rooteen routine

rope [roped]

rore roar *[lion]
raw *[fresh]

rose *[flower] rows *[boat]

rosette

rost roast

rosy

rot [rotting rotted]

rota *[list] rotor *[blade]

rotashun rotation

rotate [rotating rotated]

rotation

rote *[repeat] wrote *[pen]

rotor *[blade] rota *[list]

rotten

rough rougher roughly

round rounder roundly

roundabout

rounders

route *[way] root *[plant]

routine

row *[boat] [rowing rowed]

row *[noise] [rowed] rowdy

rownd round

rows *[boat] rose *[flower]

royal royally royalty

rub [rubbing rubbed]

rubarb rhubarb

rubber rubbery

rubbish [rubbished] rubbishy

rubble

ruby rubies

rucksack

rudder

rude ruder rudest

rude rudely rudeness

ruel rule

Rugby League Rugby Union

rugged

ruin [ruining ruined]

rule ruler [ruling ruled]
rumatic rheumatic
rumatisum rheumatism
rumble [rumbling rumbled]
rumour [rumoured]
rumple [rumpled]
run [running ran] runner
rung *[ring] wrung *[wet]
runny runnier runniest
runway
rush [rushing rushed]
Rushun Russian
russel rustle
rust rusted rusty
rustle rustler
[rustling rustled]
rut [rutted]
rute root *[plant]
route *[way]
ruthless ruthlessly
ruthlessness
ryce rice
ryme rhyme
ryval rival

sabbath

sachel — satchel

sack [sacking sacked]

sacrifice sacrificial
[sacrificing sacrificed]

sad sadder sadly sadness

sadden [saddening saddened]

saddle [saddling saddled]

safari safaris

safe safer safely

safety

saffire — sapphire

saftey — safety

sag [sagging sagged] saggy

said

saif — safe

sail *[boat]* — sale *[goods]*
[sailing sailed]

sailor

saim — same

saint saintly

saiv — save

sak — sack *[bag, destroy]*; sake *[sake of]*

sake

sakrifise — sacrifice

salad

salary salaries

sale *[goods]* — sail *[boat]*

salery — salary

sales ~man ~person ~woman

saliva

salmon

salon

salt salty saltier

salute [saluting saluted]

salvage [salvaged]

salvige — salvage

Samaritan

same sameness

samon — salmon

sample [sampling sampled]

sand [sanding sanded]

sandbank sandpit

sandwich sandwiches

sandy sandier sandiest

sane sanely saner

sanity

sank

Santa Claus

sanwich — sandwich

sapphire

sarcastic sarcastically

sardine

sari

sarkastik sarcastic
sarm psalm
sat
Satan Satanic
satchel
satellite
Saterday Saturday
satisfactory
satisfy satisfaction
[satisfying satisfied]
Saturday
sauce *[dip] source *[start]
saucepan
saucer
sauna
saunter [sauntering sauntered]
sausage
sause sauce *[liquid]
source *[origin]
savage savagely
[savaging savaged]
save [saving saved] saver
savige savage
saviour
saw *[see] soar *[fly]
sore *[hurt]
saw *[cut] [sawn] sawdust
saxophone saxophonist
say [saying said]
saym same
saynt saint
sayvyer saviour
scab scabby scabbier
scaffold scaffolding
scair scare
scald [scalding scalded]
scale [scaling scaled]
scalp [scalped]
scalpel
scaly scalier scaliest
scam
scamper [scampered]
scampi
scan [scanning scanned]
scandal scandalous
scanner
scar *[mark] scare *[shock]
scarce scarcely scarcity
scare *[shock] scar *[mark]
scarecrow
scarf scarves
scarlet
scarse scarce
scary scarier scariest
scate skate
scatter [scattering scattered]

scatty scattier scattiest
scavenge scavenger
[scavenging scavenged]
scaw score
scene *[stage] seen *[eyes]
scenery
scent *[smell] sent *[gone]
cent *[money]
scerd scared
scery scary
schedule [scheduled]
scholar scholarship
school ~boy ~child ~girl
science scientist
scientific scientifically
scill skill
scin skin
scip skip
scissors
scoff [scoffing scoffed]
scolar scholar
scold *[tell off] scald *[burn]
scone
scool school
scoop [scooped]
scoot scooter
scorch [scorching scorched]
score [scored] scoreboard

scorpion
Scot Scotch Scottish
scout [scouted]
scowl [scowling scowled]
scrabble [scrabbled]
scrach scratch
scramble [scrambled]
scrap *[junk] [scrapped]
scrape *[remove]
scratch [scratches]
[scratching scratched]
scratchy scratchier
scrawl [scrawled]
scrawny scrawnier
screach screech
scream
screech screeches
[screeching screeched]
screen screenwriter
screme scream
screw [screwed] screwdriver
screwpel scruple
scribble scribbler
[scribbling scribbled]
scribe
scripcher scripture
script scriptwriter
scripture

scroll [scrolled]

scroo — screw

scrooge

scrornee — scrawny

scrounge scrounger

scrownge — scrounge

scrub [scrubbing scrubbed]

scruff scruffy scruffier

scrum

scrunch [scrunches] [scrunching scrunched]

scuba

scuff [scuffing scuffed]

scuffle [scuffling scuffled]

sculpcher — sculpture

sculpt [sculpted]

sculptor *[artist]

sculpture *[carving]

scum scummy

scurry [scurrying scurried]

scuttle [scuttled]

scwelchey — squelchy

sea *[waves] — see *[eyes]

sea-anenome

sea ~front ~gull ~horse

sea ~shore ~sick ~side

sead — said *[say]; seed *[plant]

seak — seek *[look for]; Sikh *[religion]

seal [sealing sealed]

sealing *[fastening] — ceiling *[roof]

seam *[cloth] — seem *[appear]

sean — scene *[stage]; seen *[eyes]

search [searches searched]

searching searchlight

seasaw — seesaw

sease — cease *[stop]; seize *[grab]

season seasonal

seat [seating seated]

secendry — secondary

second secondly

secondary

secrecy

secretary secretaries

secure [secured] securely

security

sed — said

see *[eyes] [seeing saw seen] — sea *[waves]

seekrit secret
seed [seeded] seedling
seel seal
seeling ceiling
seem *[appear] seam *[cloth]
[seeming seemed]
seen *[see] scene *[stage]
seereez series
seeriul cereal
seesaw [seesawed]
seeson season
seet seat
seid said
seize *[grab] cease *[stop]
sekure secure
sekwence sequence
sekwin sequin
seldom
selebrate celebrate
select [selecting selected]
selection selective
selery celery
self selves
selfish selfishly
selfless selflessly
sell *[shop] cell *[prison]
seller *[sales person] cellar *[room]

Sellotape™
Selsius Celsius
selves
seme seam *[cloth]
seem *[appear]
sement cement
semetery cemetery
semi ~circle ~circular
semi ~colon ~conscious
semi-final
send [sending sent] sender
sene scene *[stage]
seen *[eyes]
sensashunal sensational
sensation sensational
sense senseless
sensible sensibly
sensitive sensitively
sensitivity sensitivities
sent *[gone] scent *[smell]
senta centre
sentence
sentens sentence
senter centre

sentigrade centigrade

sentimental   sentimentality
sentimetre   centimetre
sentipede   centipede
sentral   central
sentry   sentries
sentury   century
separate   seperately
separation
sepret   separate
September
sequence   sequential
sequin [sequinned]
ser   sir
seramic   ceramic
serch   search
serchin   searching
sereal   cereal *[grain]
serial *[sequence]
seremonee   ceremony
serf *[slave]   surf *[sea]
serface   surface
sergeant
sergeon   surgeon
serial *[sequence]   cereal *[grain]
serialisation [serialising]
series
serious   seriously

sermon
sername   surname
serpent
serprise   surprise
sertain   certain
sertificate   certificate
servant
serve [serving served]
service [serviced]
sesshun   session
session
set *[put]   seat *[sitting]
sett *[badger]
setentes   sentences
settee
setting
settle [settling settled]
seveir   severe
seven   seventeen   seventh
sevon   seven
seventy   seventieth
several
severe   severely   severity
sevnteen   seventeen
sevrel   several
sew *[clothes] [sewing sewn]   sow *[seed]   so *[thus]
sewer   sewerage

sewn *[clothes] sown *[seed]
sex
sey say
sfere sphere
shabby shabbier
shack
shackle [shackled]
shade shaded shady
shadow shadowy
shaft
shaggy shaggier
shaid shade
shaip shape
shair share
shake [shaking shaken]
shaky shakier
shall
shallow shallower
shamble shambles
shame *[guilt] sham *[fake]
shameful shamefully
shameless shamelessly
shampain champagne
shampoo [shampooed]
shan't [shall not]
shape shapeless shapely
shark shark-infested
sharp sharply sharpness

sharpen sharpener
[sharpening sharpened]
shatter [shattered]
shave [shaving shaved]
shaw shore *[sea]
sure *[certain]
shawl
shawt short
she she's [she is, has]
shear *[clip] sheer *[steep]
shed *[hut, hair]
she'd *[she had, would]
shedule schedule
sheep sheepish sheepishly
sheer *[steep] shear *[clip]
sheet sheeting
sheild shield
shelf shelves
shell [sea] she'll *[she will]
shelter [sheltering sheltered]
shepherd
sheriff
shert shirt
she's [she is, she has]
shi she *[female]
shy *[timid]
shield [shielding shielded]
shier sheer

shiffon chiffon

shift [shifting shifted] shifty

shimmer shimmery
[shimmering shimmered]

shin *[leg]

shine *[sun] [shining shone]

shingle shingly

shiny shinier shiniest

ship [shipping shipped]

shipwreck [shipwrecked]

shirk [shirking shirked]

shirt

shiver shivery
[shivering shivered]

sho show

shoal

shoar shore *[sea]
sure *[certain]

shock [shocking shocked]

shoddy shoddier

shoe *[foot] shoo *[away]
[shoes shoing shoed]

shoe ~horn ~lace

shofer chauffeur

shok shock

sholder shoulder

shone *[lit up, polished] shown *[did show]

shoo *[away] shoe *[foot]
[shooes shooing shooed]

shood should

shook

shool school

shoot *[target] chute *[slide]
[shooting shot]

shoow shoe

shop [shopping shopped]

shoplifter [shoplifting]

shore *[sea] sure *[certain]

shorn

short shortly shortness

shortage

shorten [shortened]

shot

should

shouldent shouldn't

shoulder

shouldn't [should not]

shout [shouting shouted]

shove [shoving shoved]

shovel [shovelling shovelled]

show [showing showed]

shower showery

showt shout

showy showier showiest

shrank

shred shredder
[shredding shredded]
shreik shriek
shrew shrewish
shrewd shrewdly
shrewdness
shriek [shrieking shrieked]
shrill shrilly
shrimp [shrimping]
shrink [shrinking shrunk]
shrivel [shrivelled]
Shrove Tuesday
shrub shrubbery
shrued shrewd
shrug [shrugging shrugged]
shrunk shrunken
shud should
shudder [shuddering shuddered]
shudent shouldn't
[should not]
shuffle shuffly
[shuffling shuffled]
shun [shunned]
shunt [shunting shunted]
shut *[close]* chute *[slide]*
[shutting shut]
shuttle
shuv shove
shuvel shovel
shy *[timid]* shyly shyness
shy *[horse]* [shies shying shied]
si sigh
siad said
Siamese
sichuayshun situation
sick *[ill]* Sikh *[religion]*
sicken [sickening sickened]
side [siding sided]
side ~burns ~ways
sider cider
sidle [sidling sidled]
sied sighed
siege
siense science
sieve [sieved]
sift [sifting sifted]
sigaret cigarette
sigh [sighing sighed]
sight *[see]* site *[place]*
sightseeing sightseer
sign signpost
signachure signature
signal [signalled]
signature
signet *[ring]* cygnet *[swan]*
significant significantly

sik sick

Sikh *[religion] seek *[look]

siksth sixth

silee silly

silence silencer
[silencing silenced]

silent silently

silhouette

silk silken silky

sillabul syllable

sillooet silhouette

silly sillier silliest

silver silvery

simbol cymbal *[music]
symbol *[sign]

simese Siamese

similar similarity

simmer [simmering]

simmetrical symmetrical

simpathetic sympathetic

simple simpler simplest

simplicity simply

simplify [simplifies]
[simplifying simplified]

simpul simple

since *[from] sins *[bad]

sincere sincerely sincerity

sindrome syndrome

sinema cinema

sinful sinfully

sing *[music] singer
[singing sang]

singe *[burn] [singeing singed]

single singly

sinister

sink [sinking sank sunk]

sinmer cinema

sinner

sinonim synonym

sinse since

sip [sipping sipped]

sir

sircul circle

sircus circus

siren

siringe syringe

sirrup syrup

sise size

sissors scissors

sissy sissies

sister sisterly

sistes sisters

sit [sitting sat]

site *[place] sight *[seeing]
siteseeing sightseeing
sitizen citizen
sitrus citrus
situate [situated]
situation
sity city
sityooashun situation
sive sieve
sivil civil
sivilisashun civilisation
six sixth
sixteen sixteenth
sixty sixtieth
size sizeable
sizzle [sizzling sizzled]
skab scab
skaffold scaffold
skale scale
skalp scalp
skaly scaly
skate [skating skated]
skateboard skateboarder
skeleton skeletal
skert skirt
sketch sketches
[sketching sketched]
sketchy sketchier

skewer [skewered]
ski *[sport] sky *[air]
[skis skiing skied]
skid *[slip] skied *[sport]
[skidding skidded]
skilful skilfully
skill [skilled]
skim [skimming skimmed]
skin [skinned]
skinny skinnier skinniest
skint
skip [skipping skipped]
skirt [skirting skirted]
skittle
skold scald *[burn]
scold *[tell off]
skon scone
skool school
skript script
skufful scuffle
skull
skuttling scuttling
skwall squall
skware square
skwobble squabble
skwod squad
skwodron squadron
skwonder squander

skwosh squash
skwot squat
sky *[space] ski *[sport]
sky ~scraper ~wards
slab
slack slacker slackest
slaiv slave
slam [slamming slammed]
slander slanderous
slang slanging match
slant [slanting slanted]
slap [slapping slapped]
slash [slashing slashed]
slate
slaughter [slaughtered]
slave slavery
slay [slaying slew slain]
sleap sleep
sleat sleet
sleave sleeve
sledge sledging
sleek sleekly sleekness
sleep [sleeping slept]
sleepless sleeplessness
sleepy sleepier sleepiest
sleet sleeting
sleeve sleeveless
slege sledge

sleigh *[snow] slay *[kill]
slender slenderness
slep sleep
slepin sleeping
slept
sley slay *[kill]
sleigh *[snow]
slice [slicing sliced]
slick slickly slickness
slide [sliding slid]
slied slide
slight slightly
slik slick
slim *[thin]
slime *[gooey] slimy
sling [slinging slung]
slip [slipping slipped]
slipper
slippery slippy slippier
slise slice
slit slitty
slither [slithered] slithery
slobber slobbery
[slobbering slobbered]
slog [slogging slogged]
slooth sleuth
slope [sloping sloped]
slorter slaughter

slot [slotting slotted]
slouch [slouching slouched]
slow slower slowly
sludge sludgy
slug sluggish sluggishly
slum slummy
slumber [slumbering slumbered]
slump [slumped]
slung
slurp [slurping slurped]
slush slushy
sly slyly slyness
slymee slimy
smack [smacking smacked]
small smaller smallest
smart smarter smartest
smartly smartness
smash [smashing smashed]
smear [smearing smeared]
smell [smelling smelt]
smelly smellier smelliest
smile [smiling smiled]
smiley smilier smiliest
smithereens
smog smoggy
smoke [smoking smoked]
smoky smokier smokiest
smooth [smoothing smoothed]
smoothie
smoothly smoothness
smother [smothering smothered]
smoulder
[smouldering smouldered]
smudge smudged smudgy
smug smugly smugness
smuggle smuggler
[smuggling smuggled]
smyle smile
snack [snacking snacked]
snaik snake
snail
snair snare
snak snack
snake [snaking] snakey
snale snail
snap [snapping snapped]
snare [snaring snared]
snarl [snarling snarled]
snatch [snatches]
[snatching snatched]
sneaky sneakier sneakiest
sneer [sneering sneered]
sneeze [sneezing sneezed]
snifel sniffle
sniff [sniffing sniffed]
sniffle [sniffling sniffled]

snigger [sniggering sniggered]
snip [snipped]
sniper
snivel [snivelling snivelled]
sno — snow
snob snobbery
snooker [snookered]
snoop [snooping snooped]
snooty
snooze [snoozing snoozed]
snorcul — snorkel
snore [snoring snored]
snorkel [snorkelling]
snort [snorting snorted]
snout
snow [snowing snowed]
snow ~ball ~boarding ~bound
snow ~drift ~drop ~fall
snow ~flake ~man ~plough
snow ~shoes ~storm
snowt — snout
snowy snowier snowiest
snub [snubbing snubbed]
snuff [snuffed]
snuffle [snuffling snuffled]
snuffly
snug snuggle snuggly
[snuggling snuggled]

snuze — snooze
so *[thus] — sew *[clothes]
sow *[seeds]
soak [soaking soaked]
soal — sole *[one]
soul *[spirit]
soap soapy soapier
soar *[fly] — saw *[see, cut]
sore *[hurt]
sob [sobbing sobbed]
soccer
social sociable socially
sock
socker — soccer
socket
soda
sodden
sofa
soffen — soften
soft softly softness
soften [softened]
software
soggy soggier soggiest
soil [soiling soiled]
sok — sock *[foot]
soak *[water]
solar
sold

solder *[metal] [soldering]

soldier *[army] [soldiering]

sole *[one] soul *[spirit]

solejur soldier

solem solemn

solemn solemnly

soler solar

solger soldier

solicitor

solid solidly

solitary

solo soloist

solt salt

solution

solve [solving solved]

som some

some *[amount] sum *[add]

some ~body ~how ~one ~thing

some ~times ~what ~where

somersault [somersaulted]

son *[boy] sun *[shine]

song

sonic

soon sooner soonest

soop soup

soor saw

soot *[coal] suit *[clothes]

soothe [soothing soothed]

sooty sootier sootiest

sopey soapy

sopping

soppy soppier soppiest

sor sore

sorce sauce *[liquid]

source *[origin]

sorcer saucer

sorcerer sorceress sorcery

sord sword

sordust sawdust

sore *[hurt] saw *[see, cut]

soar *[fly]

sorely

sorn sawn

sorna sauna

soro sorrow

sorrow sorrowful

sorrowfully

sorry sorrier sorriest

sorserer sorcerer

sort *[kind] sought *[seek]

sory sorry

soshabul sociable

soshall social

sosiety society

sossige sausage

sought *[seek] sort *[kind]

soul *[spirit] sole *[one]
sound soundly
[sounding sounded]
soundless soundlessly
soup
sour sourly sourness
source *[start] sauce *[dip]
south southern southerner
souvenir
sovereign
sovren sovereign
sow *[seed] sew *[clothes]
sow *[pig] so *[thus]
sown *[seed] sewn *[clothes]
sownd sound
sowr sour
sowth south
space [spacing spaced]
space ~man ~ship ~suit
spade
spagety spaghetti
spaghetti
spair spare
spam
span [spanning spanned]
spaner spanner
spangle [spangled]
spaniel

spank [spanking spanked]
spanner
spanyel spaniel
spare [sparing spared]
spark [sparking sparked]
sparkeling sparkling
sparkle sparkly
[sparkling sparkled]
sparrow sparrowhawk
spase space
spatter [spattering spattered]
speach speech
speak [speaking spoke]
spear spearmint
special specially
species
speckle speckled
spectacles spectacled
spectacular spectacularly
spectator
speech speechless
speed [speeding sped]
speedometer
speedy speedier speediest
speek speak
speer spear
speesheez species
spektakular spectacular

spell [spelling spelt]
spellbinding spellbound
spend [spending spent]
spensiv expensive
speshul special
sphere spherical
spice spiced spicy
spider spidery
spied
spike [spiking spiked]
spikey spikier spikiest
spill [spilling spilt]
spin *[turn] spine *[back]
[spinning spun]
spinach
spine *[back] spin *[turn]
spineless spinelessly
spinich spinach
spining spinning
spiral
spire
spise spice
spit *[saliva] [spitting spat]
spite *[nasty]
spiteful spitefully
splash [splashing splashed]
splashy splashier
splatter [splattered]

splender splendour
splendid splendidly
splendour
splinter [splintered]
split [splitting]
splodge splodgy
splutter [spluttering spluttered]
spoak spoke
spoil [spoiling spoilt]
spoiler
spoke spoken spokesman
sponge [sponging sponged]
spongy spongier spongiest
spook [spooked]
spooky spookier spookiest
spoon [spooning spooned]
spoonful
sport [sporting sported]
sporty sportier sportiest
sportsman sportswoman
spot [spotting spotted]
spotless spotlessly
spotlight [spotlit]
spotty spottier spottiest
spout [spouting spouted]
sprain
sprang
sprawl [sprawled]

spray [spraying sprayed]
spread [spreading spread]
spred — spread
spring [springing sprang sprung]
spring springtime
springy springier
sprinkle sprinkler
[sprinkling sprinkled]
sprint [sprinting sprinted]
sprinter
spritely
sprout [sprouting sprouted]
sprung
spruys — surprise
spuk — spook
spur [spurred]
spurt [spurting spurted]
sputter [sputtering sputtered]
spy [spies spying spied]
spyke — spike
spyne — spine
spyral — spiral
spyre — spire
squabble [squabbling squabbled]
squad squadron
squall squally squallier
squander
[squandering squandered]

square squarely
squash [squashing squashed]
squashy squashier
squat [squatting squatted]
squawk [squawking squawked]
squeak [squeaking squeaked]
squeaky
squeakier squeakiest
squeal [squealing squealed]
squeek — squeak
squeeze [squeezing squeezed]
squelch squelchy
[squelching squelched]
squerm — squirm
squert — squirt
squid
squiggle squiggly
squint [squinting squinted]
squirel — squirrel
squirm [squirming squirmed]
squirrel
squirt [squirting squirted]
squish [squished] squishy
squork — squawk
stab [stabbing stabbed]
stabel — stable
stabilisers
stable

stachue	statue
stack [stacking stacked]	
stadium	
staek	stake **[post]*
	steak **[beef]*
staer	stair **[step]*
	stare **[gaze]*
staff [staffing staffed]	
stag **[deer]*	
stage **[time, theatre]*	
stagger [staggering staggered]	
stagnant	
stail	stale
stain [staining stained]	
stair **[step]*	stare **[gaze]*
stait	state
stak	stack
stake **[post]*	steak **[beef]*
stalactite **[down]*	
stalagmite **[up]*	
stale stalemate	
stalegmite	stalagmite **[up]*
stalektite	stalactite **[down]*
stalk **[follow]*	stork **[bird]*
[stalking stalked]	
stalker	
stall [stalling stalled]	
stallion	
stalyen	stallion
stamp [stamping stamped]	
stampede [stampeding]	
stand [standing stood]	
stand-offish	
stane	stain
stank	
stapel	staple
staple [stapled]	stapler
star **[sky]*	stare **[gaze]*
starboard	
stare **[gaze]*	stair **[step]*
staree	starry
starlight starlit	
starling	
starred starry starrier	
start [starting started]	
startle [startling startled]	
starve starvation	
[starving starved]	
stash [stashed]	
stashun	station
state [stating stated]	
statement statesman	
station stationmaster	
stationary **[still]*	
stationery **[paper]*	

statue
stay [staying stayed]
stayje stage
steady steadier steadiest
steak *[beef] stake *[post]
steal *[take] steel *[iron]
[stealing stole stolen]
stealth stealthy
steam [steaming steamed]
steamy steamier steamiest
stedy steady
steel *[iron] steal *[take]
steep steeply steepness
steeple ~chase ~jack
steer [steering steered]
stencil stencilling
stensil stencil
step [stepping stepped]
ster stir
stern sternly sternness
stew [stewing stewed]
steward stewardess
stewdent student
stich stitch
stick [sticking stuck]
sticker
sticky stickier stickiest
stier steer

stiff stiffer stiffest
stiffen [stiffened]
stiffly stiffness
stik stick
stiky sticky
stile *[step] style *[type]
still stiller stillness
stilts
sting [stinging stung]
stingy stingier stingiest
stink [stinking stank stunk]
stir [stirring stirred]
stirrup
stitch stitches
[stitching stitched]
stoal stole
stoan stone
stoat
stocking
stodge stodgy stodgier
stole stolen
stomach stomach-ache
stomp [stomping stomped]
stone Stone Age
stony stonier stoniest
stood
stool
stoop [stooping stooped]

stop [stopping stopped]
stopper
stopt — stopped
store [storing stored]
storey *[floor] — story *[tale]
stork *[bird] — stalk *[follow]
storm stormy stormier
story *[tale] — storey *[floor]
storyteller storytelling
stout stouter stoutest
stoutly stoutness
stove
stowt — stout
straey — stray
straggle straggly [straggling straggled]
straight straighter
straightforward
straighten straightened
strain [straining strained]
strand stranded
strane — strain
strange strangely
stranger
strangle strangler [strangling strangled]
straw
strawberry strawberries

stray [straying strayed]
strayt — straight
streak streaky streakier [streaking streaked]
stream streamer [streaming streamed]
strech — stretch
streem — stream
street streetwise
strength
strengthen [strengthened]
strenth — strength
stress stressed stressful
stressfully
stretch stretches [stretching stretched]
stretcher
strict stricter strictest
strictly strictness
stride [striding strode]
strike [striking struck]
strikt — strict
string stringing stringy
stripe striped stripey
stroad — strode
strobrey — strawberry
strode
stroke [stroking stroked]

stroll [strolling strolled]
strong stronger strongly
strop stroppy stroppier
stror straw
strorbury strawberry
struck
struggle [struggling struggled]
strung
stryke strike
stub [stubbed]
stubble stubbly
stubborn stubbornly
stubbornness
stubel stubble
stuck stuck-up
student
studio
study studies [studying studied]
studyo studio
stue stew
stuff [stuffing stuffed]
stuffy stuffier stuffiest
stule stool
stumack stomach
stumble stumbled
stumok stomach
stun [stunning stunned]
stung
stunk
stupendous
stunt stuntman
stupid stupider stupidest
stupidly stupidity
stur stir
sturn stern
stutter stutterer
[stuttering stuttered]
sty sties
style *[type] stile *[step]
subdued
suberb suburb *[town]
superb *[great]
subject
submarine submariner
submerge [submerged]
submurje submerge
subset
substance
substantial substantially
substence substance
substitute substitution
[substituting substituted]
subtract subtraction
[subtracting subtracted]
suburb suburban suburbia
subzero

succeed [succeeding succeeded]
success successes
successful successfully
such
suck [sucking sucked]
sucseed succeed
sucsess success
suction
sudden suddenly
sudenley suddenly
suede *[leather] swayed *[moved]
sueur sewer *[drain]
sure *[certain]
suffer sufferer
[suffering suffered]
sufficient sufficiently
suffix suffixes
suffocate suffocation
[suffocating suffocated]
suffragette
sufishent sufficient
sufokate suffocate
sugar sugary
suggest [suggesting suggested]
suggestion
suit
suitable suitably
sulen sullen

sulk [sulking sulked] sulkily
sulky sulkier sulkiest
sullen sullenly sullenness
sultan
sultana
sum *[add] some *[amount]
sumer summer
sumersorlt somersault
sumery summary *[short]
summery *[warm]
summarise [summarised]
summary *[outline] summery *[warm]
summer summertime
summit
sumthing something
sun *[shine] son *[boy]
sun ~bathe ~burn ~burnt
sun ~flower ~glasses ~lit
sun ~light ~rise ~screen
sun ~set ~shine ~stroke
sun ~tan ~tanned
sundae *[ice cream]
Sunday *[day of week]
sune soon
sung

sunk   sunken
sunny   sunnier   sunniest
super *[fab]   supper *[meal]
superb   superbly
superhero
superhuman
superior   superiority
supermarket
supersonic
supervise   supervisor
[supervising supervised]
supervision
suply   supply
suport   support
supose   suppose
supper *[meal]   super *[fab]
suppervise   supervise
supply   supplies
[supplying supplied]
support   supportive
[supporting supported]
suppose   supposedly
[supposing supposed]
supprise   surprise
sure *[certain]   shore *[sea]
surely
surender   surrender
surf *[sea]   serf *[slave]

surface   surfaces
[surfacing surfaced]
surge [surging surged]
surgeon
surgery   surgeries
surgical   surgically
surly
surmon   sermon
surname
suround   surround
surpent   serpent
surpliing   supplying
surprise   surprisingly
[surprising surprised]
surrender   surrendered
surround   surroundings
[surrounding surrounded]
survalence   surveillance
survant   servant
surve   serve
surveillance
survey   surveyor
[surveying surveyed]
survice   service
surviet   serviette
survival   survivor
survive [surviving survived]
suspect [suspecting suspected]

suspend [suspended]
suspense
suspicion suspicious
suspiciously
sutch such
sute soot *[coal]
suit *[clothes]
sutibul suitable
suvenear souvenir
swade suede
swagger [swaggering swaggered]
swallow swallowed
swam
swamp swamped swampy
swan [swanning swanned]
swap [swapping swapped]
swarm *[bees] swam *[swim]
swat *[hit] swot *[study]
sway [swaying swayed]
swayd suede
sweat *[hot] sweet *[food]
[sweating sweated]
sweater
sweaty sweatier sweatiest
swede *[vegetable]
Swede *[from Sweden]
sweep sweeper [sweeping swept]
sweet sweetly sweetness

sweeten sweetened sweetener
swept
swerve [swerving swerved]
swet sweat *[hot]
sweet *[food]
swetter sweater
swich switch
swift swiftly swiftness
swim swimmer
[swimming swam swum]
swine
swing
swipe [swiping swiped]
switch [switches switching switched]
swivel [swivelling swivelled]
swollen
swollow swallow
swomp swamp
swon swan
swoop [swooping swooped]
swop swap
sword ~fish ~sman
swot *[study] swat *[hit]
swum
swung
swurve swerve
swyne swine
swype swipe

sycul	cycle

syclist	cyclist
syclone	cyclone
sygn	sign
sylens	silence
sylent	silent
sylinder	cylinder
syllable	syllabic
syllabus
symbol *[sign]	cymbal *[music]

symmetrical
sympathetic	sympathetically
sympathise
[sympathising sympathised]
sympathy
syncere	sincere
synonym
syrup	syrupy
systematic	systematically
syte	cite *[quote]
sight *[seeing]
site *[place]

T-shirt
tabby
tabel table
tabelspoon tablespoon
table tablecloth
tablespoon tablespoonful
tablet
tabloid
tac take
tack *[nail] take *[get]
tackle [tackling tackled]
tacks *[pins] tax *[money]
tacky tackier tackiest
tact tactful tactfully
tactic tactical
tactless tactlessly
tadpole
taek take
tag [tagging tagged]
t'ai chi
tail *[dog] tale *[story]
taip tape
tair tear
take [taking took taken]
takeaway takeover
takul tackle
taks tax
taksi taxi
takt tact
taktik tactic
tale *[story] tail *[dog]
talen talon
talent talented
talk [talking talked]
talkative
tall taller tallest
talon
tame [taming tamed]
tamper [tampering tampered]
tan [tanning tanned]
tang tangy
tangerine
tangle [tangled]
tanjerine tangerine
tank
tannoy
tantrum
tap [tapping tapped]
tap-dance tap-dancing
tape [taping taped]
tapestry tapestries
tapistry tapestry
tar [tarred]
tarantula
target [targeting targeted]
tarmac

tarnish [tarnished]
tart tartness
tartan
task [tasked]
tassel [tasselled]
taste [tasting tasted]
tasteful tastefully
tasty tastier tastiest
tattered tatters
tattoo tattoos
tatty tattier tattiest
tatu tattoo
taught *[teach] taut *[tight]
taunt [taunting taunted]
Taurus
taut *[tight] taught *[teach]
tawn torn
tawny
tax [taxes taxing taxed]
taxi taxis
tea *[drink] tee *[golf]
teach [teaches teaching taught]
teacher
team *[group] teem *[swarm]
teanage teenage
teapot teaspoon teatowel
tear *[cry] tier *[layer]
tear *[rip] [tearing torn]

tearful tearfully
tease [teasing teased]
Teashert T-shirt
teaspoon teaspoonful
techer teacher
technical technically
technician
technique
technology
teddy teddies
tedious
tedy teddy
tee *[golf] tea *[drink]
[tees teeing teed]
teef teeth
teejuncshun T-junction
teem *[swarm] team *[group]
teenage teenager teens
teese tease
Teeshert T-shirt
teespoon teaspoon
teeter [teetering teetered]
teeth *[mouth] teething
teethe *[grow teeth]
tef teeth
tekneek technique
tekst text
telefone telephone

telephone telephonist
[telephoning telephoned]
telescope telescopic
televise [televised]
television
telivise televise
telivizhun television
tell [telling told] teller telltale
telly
temper temperamental
temperature
temple
temporary
tempracher temperature
tempramentl temperamental
tempt [tempting tempted]
tempul temple
tempur temper
ten tenth
tenant
tend [tended] tendency
tender tenderly tenderness
tendon
tendur tender
tenent tenant
tener tenner *[£10]
tenor *[sing]
tenner

tennis
tenor
tenpin bowling
tense [tensed] tensely
tenshun tension
tension
tent
tentacle
tenth
tepid
terban turban
terer terror
tererise terrorise
tereybul terrible
terier terrier
terific terrific
teriss terrace
teritoriel territorial
terkey turkey
term [termed]
terminal terminally
terminate termination
[terminating terminated]
termoil turmoil

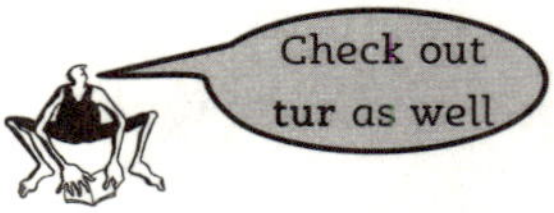

terning turning

ternip turnip
terodactil pterodactyl
teror terror
terqwoys turquoise
terrace terraced
terracotta
terrapin
terrestrial
terrible terribly
terrier
terrific terrifically
terrify [terrifies]
[terrifying terrified]
territorial
territory territories
terror terrorism
terrorise terrorist
[terrorising terrorised]
tertle turtle
test [testing tested]
testify [testifies testifying testified]
tether [tethering tethered]
Tewder Tudor
tewlip tulip
tewn tune
Tewsday Tuesday
text [texting texted]
texture

tey tea
thach thatch
than

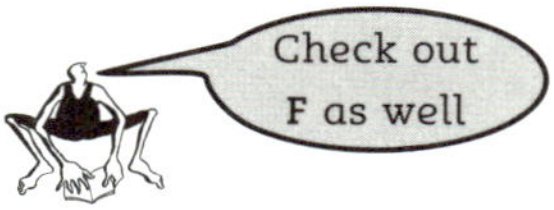

thank [thanking thanked]
thankful thankfully
thankless thanklessly
thank you
that
thatch [thatched]
thaw [thawing thawed]
thay they
the
theat that
theatre theatrical
theef thief
thees these
theft
their *[own] there *[place]
theirs *[owns] there's *[there is]
theis these
them themselves
theme [themed]
then
theory theories
ther there

therapy therapist
there *[place] their *[own]
they're *[they are]
therefore
there's *[there is] theirs *[owns]
therfour therefore
thermometer
thers there's *[there is]
theirs *[owns]
Thersday Thursday
thes these
these
they
they'd [they had, would]
they'll [they will, shall]
they're *[they are] there *[place]
their *[own]
they've [they have]
thick thicker thickest
thicken [thickening thickened]
thicket
thickly thickness
thief thieves
thier there *[place]
their *[own]
thigh
thik thick

thimble thimbleful
thin thinner thinnest
thing
think thinker [thinking thought]
thinly thinness
thir their
third thirdly
thirst thirsty thirstier
thirteen thirteenth
thirty thirtieth
this
thistle
thogh though
thore thaw
thorn thorny thornier
thorough thoroughly
thoroughbred
thoroughness
thort thought
thorteen fourteen
thortless thoughtless
those
though
thought thought-provoking
thoughtful thoughtfully
thoughtfulness
thoughtless thoughtlessly
thoughtlessness

thousand thousandth
thow though
thowsand thousand
thrash [thrashing thrashed]
thread threadbare
[threading threaded]
threat
threaten [threatening threatened]
thred thread
three three-dimensional
thret threat
thretton threaten
threw *[ball] through *[via]
thrill [thrilling thrilled]
thrive [thriving thrived throve]
throat throaty
throb [throbbing throbbed]
throne *[king] thrown *[ball]
throng [thronging thronged]
throo through
throttle [throttled]
through *[via] threw *[ball]
throughout
throw *[ball] through *[via]
[throwing threw thrown]
thrown *[ball] throne *[king]
thrush thrushes
thrust [thrusting thrust]

thud [thudding thudded]
thum thumb
thumb [thumbing thumbed]
thump [thumping thumped]
thunder thundery
[thundering thundered]
thurmometur thermometer
Thursday
thus
thwart [thwarted]
thwort thwart
thyme *[herb] time *[clock]
tiara
tic *[twitch] tick *[clock, mark]
[ticking ticked]
ticket
tickle ticklish [tickling tickled]
tidal
tiddlywinks
tide *[sea] tied *[up]
tidy tidier tidiest
tie *[up] Thai *[Thailand]
tie [ties tying tied]
tie chee t'ai chi
tied *[up] tide *[sea]
tier *[layer] tear *[cry]
tire *[sleep]
tyre *[wheel]

tifoon typhoon
tifoyd typhoid
tiger tigress
tight tighter tightly
tighten [tightening tightened]
tik tick
tikul tickle
tile
till *[until, shop]
tilt [tilting tilted]
timber
time *[clock] thyme *[herb]
[timing timed]
time ~less ~table
timid timidity timidly
tin tinned
tinge [tinged]
tingle [tingling tingled]
tinker [tinkering tinkered]
tinkle [tinkling tinkled]
tinsel tinselly
tint [tinting tinted]
tiny tinier tiniest
tip *[advice] type *[sort]
tiperiter typewriter
tipes types
tipical typical
tiptoe [tiptoeing tiptoed]

tirannosaurus tyrannosaurus
tirant tyrant
tire *[sleep] tyre *[wheel]
tire [tiring tired]
tireless tirelessly
tirn turn
tirteen thirteen
tishue tissue
tissue
tit *[bird] tight *[firm]
titbit
tite tight
title [titled]
titter [tittering tittered]
tiyed tired
to *[do] too *[also]
two *[number]
toad *[frog] towed *[pulled]
toadstool
toan tone
toast [toasted]
tobacco tobacconist
toboggan
[tobogganing tobogganed]
today
toddle [toddling toddled] toddler
tode toad *[frog]
towed *[pulled]

todel toddle
toe *[foot] tow *[pull]
toffee toffees
toga
together togetherness
toil [toiling toiled]
toilet toiletries
token
toksic toxic
told
toled told
tolerable tolerably
tolerait tolerate
tolerance tolerant
tolerate [tolerating tolerated]
toll [tolling tolled]
tolrabul tolerable
tom ~boy ~cat
tomato tomatoes
tomb tombstone
tombola
tomeake tummy ache
tommow tomorrow
tomorrow
ton *[imperial] tonne *[metric]
tone toneless
tongs
tongue
tonic
tonight
tonne *[metric] ton *[imperial]
tonsil tonsilitis
too *[also] to *[do]
two *[2]
tooc took
toocan toucan
toogever together
took
tool toolkit
toom tomb
toopay toupée
toot [tooting tooted]
tooth ~ache ~brush
tooth ~less ~paste ~pick
toothy
tootifrooti tutti-frutti
top [topping topped]
topic topical
topple [toppled]
topsy-turvy
torch torchlight
torcher torture
torist tourist
tork talk
torment tormentor
[tormenting tormented]

torn
tornado tornadoes
tornament tournament
torney tawny
tornt taunt
torpedo torpedoes
[torpedoing torpedoed]
torrent torrential
Torrus Taurus
tortoise tortoiseshell
tortoys tortoise
torture torturer
[torturing tortured]
tortuss tortoise
Tory Tories
toss [tossing tossed]
tost toast
total totally
totem pole
totter [tottering tottered]
toucan
touch [touches touching touched]
touchy touchier touchiest
tough tougher toughest
toughen [toughened]
toughness
toupée
tour *[journey] tore *[rip]
tourist touristy tourism
tournament
Tousday Tuesday
tow *[pull] toe *[foot]
[towing towed]
toward towards
towed *[pulled] toad *[frog]
towel towelling
tower [towering towered]
towle towel
town
toxic toxin
toy
toylet toilet
trabl trouble
trace traceable tracing
track [tracking tracked]
tractor
trade [trading traded]
tradesman
tradishun tradition
tradition traditional
traffic
tragedy tragedies
tragic tragically
traid trade
trail [trailing trailed]
train trainer [training trained]

trais trace
traitor
trajedy tragedy
trajic tragic
trak track
trale trail
tram
tramp [tramped]
trample [trampled]
trampoline trampolining
trance
trane train
tranquil tranquility
tranquilliser [tranquillised]
transatlantic
transe trance
transfer [transferring transferred]
transform transformation
[transforming transformed]
transishun transition
transition
translate translation
[translating translated]
transmishun transmission
transmission
transmit [transmitted]
transparent transparency
transplant [transplanted]

transport [transported]
trap [trapping trapped]
trapeze
trapezium trapezoid
trash trashed trashy
trauma traumatic
travel traveller
[travelling travelled]
travler traveller
trawler
tray
traytor traitor
treacherous treacherously
treachery
treacle
tread [treading trod trodden]
treason treasonable
treasure treasurer
[treasuring treasured]
treasury
treat [treating treated]
treatment
treaty treaties
treble
trecherus treacherous
trechery treachery
tred tread
tree trees

treeo trio
treet treat
treety treaty
trek [trekking trekked]
tremble [trembling trembled]
tremendous tremendously
tremor
trench trenches
trend trendy trendier
treshere treasure
trespass trespasses
trew true
trewansy truancy
trewly truly
trewthful truthful
trial
triangle triangular
triathlon
tribal tribe tribes
tributary tributaries
tribute
triceps
trick [tricked] trickery
trickle [trickling trickled]
tricky trickier trickiest
tricycle
tried
trifle

triggard triggered
trigger [triggered]
triing trying
trik trick
trikel trickle
trile trial
trilogy
trim [trimming trimmed]
trio
trip [tripping tripped]
tripet tripped
triple triplets
triseps triceps
triumph triumphant
trivial
troble trouble
trod trodden
trofee trophy
troff trough
troll
trolley trollies
trombone trombonist
troop [trooping trooped]
trophy trophies
tropic tropical
trorma trauma
trot [trotting trotted]
trouble [troubling troubled]

troublemaker troublesome
trough
trousers
trout
trowel
trowser trouser
truancy truant
trubbel trouble
truce
truck trucker trucking
trudge [trudging trudged]
true
truj trudge
truly
trumpet [trumpeted]
truncheon
trundle [trundling trundled]
trunk
trupeez trapeze
trust [trusting trusted]
trustworthy trusty
truth truthful truthfully
truthfulness
try [tries trying tried]
trycycle tricycle
tryed tried
tryumf triumph
tsar tsarina

T-shirt
tsunami tsunamis
tub tubby tubbier
tube tubular
tuberculosis
tuch touch
tuck [tucking tucked]
tuct tucked
Tudor
Tuesday
tuffen toughen
tuft tufted tufty
tug [tugging tugged]
tuition
tuk took *[take]*
tuck *[in]*
tule tool
tulip
tumble [tumbling tumbled]
tume tomb
tummy tummyache
tumour
tumy tummy
tuna
tune [tuning tuned]
tuneful tunefully
tung tongue
tunic

tunnel tunneller
[tunnelling tunnelled]
tupay toupée
turban
turbulence turbulent
turf [turfed]
turkey *[bird]*
Turkey *[country]* Turkish
turm term

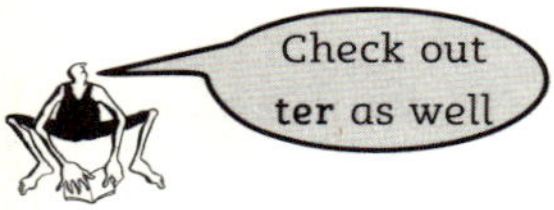

turmoil
turn [turning turned]
turnip
turquoise
turrestrial terrestrial
turret
turtle turtledove
Tusday Tuesday
tusk
tussle [tussling tussled]
tuth tooth
tutor tutorial
tutti-frutti
tuword toward
twang [twanging twanged]
tweak [tweaking tweaked]
tweed tweedy
tweek tweak
tweet [tweeting]
tweezers
twelth twelfth
twelve twelfth
twente twenty
twentieth
twenty twenty-first
twerl twirl
twevl twelve
twice
twiddle [twiddling twiddled]
twig [twigged]
twilight
twin *[two]* [twinned]
twine *[string]* [twined]
twinge [twinged]
twinkle [twinkling twinkled]
twirl [twirling twirled]
twise twice
twist [twisting twisted]
twisty twistier twistiest
twit
twitch twitches twitchy
[twitching twitched]
twitter twittery
[twittering twittered]

two *[2]	to *[in order to]
	too *[also, very]
twurl	twirl
twylight	twilight
ty	tie
tyara	tiara
tyde	tide *[sea]
	tied *[up]
tying	
tyme	time *[clock]
	thyme *[herb]
type	

typewriter typist
[typing typed]
typhoon
typhoid
typical typically
tyrannise [tyrannised]
tyrannosaurus rex
tyrant

tyre *[wheel]	tire *[sleep]
tytan	tighten

ubout about
udder
uftaer after
ugane again
ugh
ugly uglier ugliest
ule Yule
uliteration alliteration
ulser ulcer
ultraviolet
umbrella
umpire *[game] [umpired] empire *[lands]
unable *[not able] enable *[to make able]
unacceptable
unaccompanied
unaccustomed
unaided
unappetising
unarmed
unaversil universal
unavoidable
unaware
unbearable unbearably
unbelievable unbelievably
unblock [unblocking unblocked]
uncertain uncertainly

uncertainty
unchanged
uncivilised
uncle
unconscious unconsciously
unconsciousness
uncontrollable
uncontrollably
unconvincing
uncover [uncovering uncovered]
undecided
undeniable undeniably
under ~cover ~graduate
under ~ground ~growth ~hand
under ~neath ~study ~wear
underestimate
underline [underlined]
undermine [undermined]
understand [understanding understood]
understandable
understandably
undertake undertaker [undertaking undertook undertaken]
undesirable
undignified
undiniabel undeniable
undo [undoing undid undone]

undoubted undoubtedly
undrinkable
unearth unearthly
[unearthing unearthed]
uneasy uneasier
uneatable uneaten
unecessary — unnecessary
uneducated
uneek — unique
unekspected — unexpected
unemotional
unemployable
unemployed unemployment
unenthusiastic
unequal unequally
unequalled
unerth — unearth
uneven unevenly
unexciting
unexpected unexpectedly
unfair unfairly unfairness
unfaithful
unfamiliar
unfashionable unfashionably
unfernished — unfurnished
unfinished
unflattering
unforeseeable
unforgettable
unforgivable
unfortunate unfortunately
unfrendly — unfriendly
unfriendly
unfurnished
ungarded — unguarded
ungrateful ungratefully
unhappiness unhappily
unhappy unhappier unhappiest
unhealthy unhealthier
unheard of
unien — union
unicorn
uniform
unimaginable
unimportant
uninhabited
unintentional
unintentionally
unintresting — uninteresting
uninterested uninteresting
union *[join] — onion *[veg]
Union Jack
unique uniquely uniqueness
unisex
unit
unite [uniting united]

unity

universal universally

universe

university universities

unjust unjustly

unkind unkinder unkindest

unkindly unkindness

unkle uncle

unknown unknowingly

unleaded

unless

unlike unlikely

unlovable unloved

unlucky unluckiest

unmanned

unmarked

unmistakable unmistakably

unmoved

unnatural unnaturally

unnecessary

unnown unknown

unpaid

unpleasant unpleasantly

unpleasantness

unplug [unplugged]

unpopular unpopularity

unprepared

unpripared unprepared

unprotected

unraliabul unreliable

unrap unwrap

unravel [unravelling unravelled]

unreal unrealistic

unreasonable unreasonably

unreliable

unritten unwritten

unruly unrulier unruliest

unscramble [unscrambled]

unscrew [unscrewing unscrewed]

unsed unsaid

unseen

unselfish unselfishly

unselfishness

unsertain uncertain

unshakeable

unsientific unscientific

unsightly

unsivilised uncivilised

unskilled

unskrew unscrew

unsociable

unsolved

unsoshabul unsociable

unspeakable

unspoken

unsporting

unsteady unsteadily
unsuccessful
unsuccessfully
unsuitable unsuited
untidy untidier untidiest
untie [untying untied]
until
untold
untrustworthy
untruthful
unusable
unusual unusually
unuther — another
unwelcome unwelcoming
unwrap [unwrapping unwrapped]
unwritten
unyun — onion *[veg]
union *[flag]
unyvers — universe
unzip [unzipping unzipped]
up ~beat ~right
upbringing
upgrade [upgraded]
upheaval
upheval — upheaval
uplift [uplifting uplifted]
upon
upper
uprising
uprite — upright
uproar
upset [upsetting]
upshot
upside-down
upstairs
uptight
uptite — uptight
upward upwards
upwood — upward
uranium
Uranus
urban
urchin
Urdu
ure — your
urge [urging urged]
urgent urgently urgency
urine
urly — early

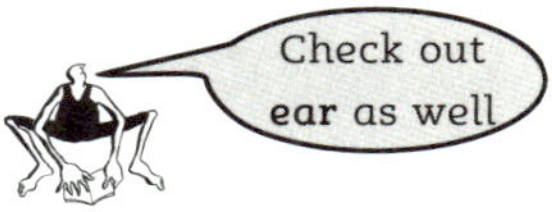

urn *[vase] — earn *[money]
urnest — earnest
Uropean — European
urth — earth

us

use [using used]   user

usable   usage

useful   usefully   usefulness

useless   uselessly

uselessness

userp   usurp

usher [ushering ushered]

uskt   asked

usual   usually

usurp [usurped]   usurper

utensil

uther   other

utmost

utter [uttering uttered]

utterly

uver   other

uvm   oven

uway   away

uze   use

uzual   usual

V-neck V-necked
vacancy vacancies
vacant vacantly
vaccinate vaccination
[vaccinating vaccinated]
vacuum [vacuuming vacuumed]
vael vale *[valley]
veil *[cloth]
vage vague
vague vaguely vagueness
vain *[proud] vein *[blood]
vane *[weather]
vaiporise vaporise
vakansy vacancy
vakant vacant
vaksinate vaccinate
vaksine vaccine
vakuum vacuum
valay valley
valentine
valew value
valley valleys
valuable
value values
valuntine valentine
valve
valyu value
vampire

van
vandal vandalism
vandalise [vandalised]
vane *[weather] vain *[proud]
vein *[blood]
vanilla
vanish [vanishing vanished]
vanity
vaper vapour
vaporise [vaporised]
vapour
variable
varied
variety varieties
various variously
varnish [varnishing varnished]
varse vase
vary *[change] very *[much]
[varying varied]
vase
vast vastly vastness
Vatican
vault
vayn vain *[proud]
vane *[weather]
vein *[blood]
veal
vector

vegetable

vegetarian veggie

vegetation

vegtabul vegetable

vehicle

veikel vehicle

veil *[cloth] vale *[valley]

vein *[blood] vain *[proud]

vane *[weather]

veiw view

vejetabul vegetable

vejetarian vegetarian

velocity

velvet velvety

vencher venture

vendetta

vending machine

vendor

venew venue

Venn diagram

venom venomous

vent [venting vented]

ventilate [ventilating ventilated]

ventilation ventilator

ventriloquist

venture [venturing ventured]

venue

venum venom

Venus

veray very

verb verbal verbally

verbalise

vercabulary vocabulary

verdict

verge

veriety variety

verius various

vermin

verruca verrucas

verse

verses *[poem] versus *[against]

version

versus *[against] verses *[poem]

vertebra vertebrae

vertebrate

vertex vertices

vertical vertically

vertigo

vertu virtue

vertual virtual

vertuos virtuous

very *[much] vary *[change]

vessel

vest

vet veterinary

veteran

veto vetoes [vetoed]
via
vialens violence
vibe vibration
vibrate [vibrating vibrated]
vicar vicarage
vice vice-president
vice versa
vicious viciously
victim
victimise [victimising victimised]
victor
Victorian
victorious victoriously
victory victories
video videos
vidio video
vielence violence
view [viewing viewed]
vigger vigour
vigilance
vigilant vigilantly
vigorous vigorously
vigour
vikar vicar
Viking
viksen vixen
viktim victim
viktimise victimise
vile
vilense violence
vilige village
villa
village villager
villain villainous villainy
vinager vinegar
vinaigrette
vine vineyard
vinegar vinegary
vintage
violence violent violently
violet
violin violinist
viper
virb verb

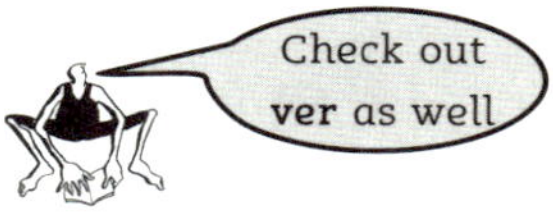

virge verge
virgin
Virgo
virjin virgin
virse verse
virtual virtually
virtue virtuous
virus viruses

visa
visable visible
vishus vicious
visible visibility visibly
vision
visit [visiting visited]
visitor
visor
visual visually
visualise visualisation
[visualising visualised]
vital vitality vitally
vitamin
vivid vividly vividness
vixen
vniler vanilla
voat vote
vocabulary
vocal vocalist vocally
vocation vocational
voice [voicing voiced]
void
vokabulary vocabulary
volcano volcanoes volcanic
vole
volkano volcano
volley volleyball
volnteerd volunteered
volt voltage
volume
voluntary voluntarily
volunteer [volunteered]
vomit [vomiting vomited]
vorlt vault
vote [voting voted]
vouch vouched voucher
vow [vowing vowed]
vowel
voyage voyager
voys voice
vue view
vulcher vulture
vulgar
vulnerable
vulture
vunrabel vulnerable
vurb verb

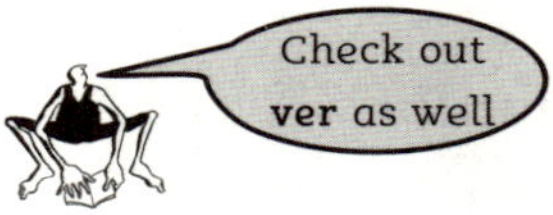

vurge verge
vurse verse
vurtuel virtual
vya via

wack whack
wacks wax
wad *[pad] wade *[water]
waddle [waddling waddled]
wade *[water] weighed *[load]
[wading waded]
wafer wafer-thin
waffle
wag [wagging wagged]
wage [waging waged]
wager
waggle [waggling waggled]
wagon
waht what
waid wade *[water]
weighed *[load]
waifer wafer
wail *[cry] whale *[sea]
[wailing wailed]
waist *[body] waste *[misuse]
waist ~band ~coat ~line
wait *[delay] weight *[load]
[waiting waited]
waiter waitress
waiting room
waj wage
wake [waking woke woken]
wakeful
waken [wakening wakened]
waks wax
Wales *[place] whales *[sea]
walk [walking walked]
walk ~about ~over ~way
walker
walkie-talkie
wall [walled]
wallaby wallabies
wallet
wallop [walloping walloped]
wallow [wallowing wallowed]
walnut
walrus walruses
waltz waltzes
wand
wander *[roam] wonder *[think]
[wandering wandered]
want [wanting wanted]
war *[battle] wore *[dress]
war ~fare ~like ~ship ~time
ward [warding warded]
warden
wardrobe
warehouse [warehousing]
wares *[goods] wears *[coat]
warm [warming warmed]
warm-hearted

warmth   warmly
warn *[alert]   worn *[old]
[warning warned]
warren
warrior
wart   warthog
wary   warier   wariest
was
wash [washing washed]
wash   ~basin ~out ~room
washer   washing
wasn't [was not]
wasp   waspish
wastage
waste *[misuse]   waist *[body]
wasteful   wastefully
wasteland
watch [watches watching watched]
watch   ~dog ~man
watchful   watchfully
water [watering watered]
water   ~colour ~cress ~fall
water   ~front ~logged
water   ~melon ~side ~tight
waterproof [waterproofed]
water-ski   water-skiing
watery
watt *[power]   what *[?]

watter   water
wave [waving waved]
wave   ~band ~length
wavy   wavier   waviest
wax [waxes waxing waxed]
waxwork
way *[track]   weigh *[load]
waykn   waken
wayt   wait *[delay]
weight *[load]
we *[us]   wee *[tiny]
weak *[feeble]   week *[7 days]
weaken
[weakening weakened]
weaker   weakest
weakly *[feebly]   weekly *[every week]
weakness
weal *[mark]   wheel *[car]
we'll *[we will, shall]
wealth
wealthy wealthier wealthiest
weapon
wear *[dress]   were *[be]
where *[place]
weir *[dam]
wearily   weariness

weard — weird

wears *[coat] — wares *[goods]

weary wearier weariest

weasel

weather *[sun, rain] — whether *[if]
[weathering weathered]

weather-beaten

weave *[cloth] — we've *[we have]
[weaving wove woven]

webbed

we'd *[we had, would] — weed *[plant]

wed *[married]

wedding

Wedensday — Wednesday

wedge [wedging wedged]

Wednesday

weed *[plant] — we'd *[we had, would]
[weeding weeded]

weedy weedier weediest

week *[7 days] — weak *[feeble]

weekend

weekly *[every week]
weakly *[feebly]

weel — weal *[mark]
wheel *[car]

weep [weeping wept]

weesal — weasel

weet — wheat

weeze — wheeze

weigh *[load] — way *[track]

weight *[load] — wait *[delay]

weight weightless

weightlessness

weight ~lifter ~lifting

weight training

weild — wield

weir *[dam] — wear *[dress]

weird weirder weirdest

weirdly weirdness

wej — wedge

welcome [welcoming welcomed]

weld [welding welded]

welfare

well better best

well-behaved

well-known

well-mannered

wellington boot

welth — wealth

wen — when

Wensday — Wednesday

went

wept

werd — weird *[strange]
word *[speech]

were *[be] whirr *[sound]
we're *[we are] weir *[dam]
weren't [were not]
werewolf werewolves
werk work
werl whirl
werld world
werr were *[be]
whirr *[sound]
west ~bound ~erly ~ern
westwards
wet [wetting wetted]
wet wetness
wether weather *[sun]
whether *[if]
we've *[we have] weave *[cloth]
whack [whacking whacked]
whacks *[hits] wax *[candle]
whale *[sea] wail *[cry]
whaling
what *[?] watt *[power]
what whatever
whatsoever
wheat
wheel *[car] weal *[mark]
[wheeling wheeled]
wheel ~barrow ~chair

wheeze wheezy
[wheezing wheezed]
when whenever
whent went
wher where
where *[place] wear *[dress]
were *[be]
whereabouts
whereas
whereupon
wherever
whether *[if] weather *[sun]
whey *[milk] way *[track]
which *[?] witch *[hag]
whichever
whiff
while whilst
whim
whimper [whimpering whimpered]
whine *[moan] wine *[drink]
whined *[moaned] wind *[turn]
whip *[beat] [whipping whipped]
whippet
whirl [whirling whirled]
whirl ~pool ~wind
whirr *[sound] were *[be]
[whirring whirred]

whisk [whisking whisked]
whisker whiskery
whisper [whispering whispered]
whistle [whistling whistled]
white whiter whitest
whitish whiteness
whiz [whizzes whizzing whizzed]
who *[?] hew *[cut]
who'd *[who had, would]
whoever
whole *[full] hole *[gap]
whole ~food ~hearted ~meal
who'll *[who will]
wholly *[fully] holy *[God]
holey *[holes]
whom whomever
whood would
whooping cough
whopper whopping
who're *[who are]
who's *[who is, has]
whose *[belongs]
who've *[who have]
why
wi why
wich which *[?]
witch *[hag]
wicked wickeder wickedest

wickedly wickedness
wicket ~keeper
wide wider widest
widely
widen [widening widened]
widespread
widow widower
width
wield [wielding wielded]
wier weir *[dam]
we're *[we are]
wierd weird
wiery weary
wife wives
wig
wiggle [wiggling wiggled]
wiggly
wigwam
wikid wicked
wild wilder wildest
wilderness wildernesses
wildly wildness
wilful wilfully wilfulness
will
willing willingly willingness
willow willowy
wilt [wilting wilted]
wily wilier wiliest

wim — whim
wimen — women
wimper — whimper
win [winning won]
wince [wincing winced]
winch [winches]
[winching winched]
wind *[turn] — whined
[winding wound] — *[moaned]
wind *[air]
wind ~fall ~mill ~pipe
wind ~screen ~surfer
window ~pane
windy windier windiest
wine *[drink] — whine *[moan]
wing [winged]
wing wingspan
wink [winking winked]
winner winnings
winter ~time
wintry
wipe [wiping wiped]
wiper
wire [wiring wired]
wire wireless
wirlwind — whirlwind
wisdom
wise wiser wisest

wisell — whistle
wisely
wish [wishing wished]
wishful wishfully
wisk — whisk
whisker
wisp wispy
wisper — whisper
wistful wistfully
wit
witch *[hag] — which *[?]
witchcraft witches
with within
wither [withering withered]
without
witness [witnessed]
witnesses
witty wittier wittiest
wizard wizardry
wnet — went
wobble [wobbling wobbled]
wobbly
woch — watch

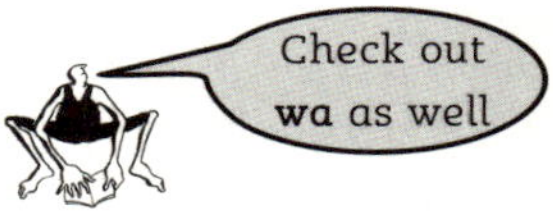

wod — wad *[pad]
word *[speech]

woffel — waffle
woft — waft
woke woken
wolf wolves
wollaby — wallaby
wollet — wallet
wollop — wallop
wollow — wallow
woltz — waltz
woman women
womb
won *[victory] one *[number]
wond — wand
wonder *[think] wander *[roam]
[wondering wondered]
wonderful wonderfully
wons — once
wont — want
won't *[will not]
wood *[trees] would *[would go]
wooded
wooden
woodlouse
wood ~land ~pecker ~wind
wood ~work ~worm
wool woollen woolly
woom — womb
wopper — whopper

wor — war *[battle]
wore *[clothes]
word [wording worded]
word-processor
wordy wordier wordiest
wore *[clothes] war *[hit]
work [working worked]
workable
work ~load ~man ~shop
workitorkie — walkie-talkie
worl — wall
worlrus — walrus
world worldwide
World War I
World War II
worm [worming wormed]
worn *[used] warn *[alert]
worpt — warped
worrant — warrant
worrior — warrior
worry [worries worrying worried]
wors — wars
worse worst
worsen [worsening worsened]
worship
[worshipping worshipped]
worst
wort — wart

worter — water

worth worthless worthwhile

worthy worthier worthiest

wos — was

wosh — wash

wosnt — wasn't

wosp — wasp

wot — watt *[power]
what *[?]

wotch — watch

would *[would go] — wood *[trees]

wouldn't *[would not]

wound *[hurt]
[wounding wounded]

wove woven

wow

wownd — wound *[clock]

woz — was

wrap *[pack] — rap *[pop, knock]
[wrapping wrapped]

wreath

wreck [wrecking wrecked]

wreckage

wren

wrench [wrenches]
[wrenching wrenched]

wrestle wrestler
[wrestling wrestled]

wretch *[rogue] — retch *[sick]

wretched wretches

wriggle [wriggling wriggled]

wriggly

wrighting — writing

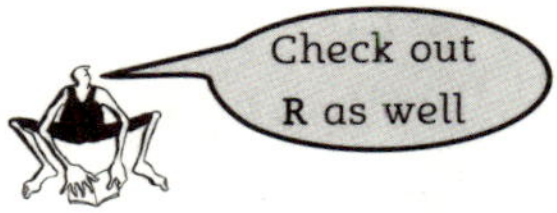

wring *[wet] — ring *[circle, bell]
[wringing wrung]

wrinkle wrinkled wrinkly

wrist wristwatch

write *[pen] — right *[exact]
rite *[act]

writer [writing wrote written]

writhe [writhing writhed]

wrong wrongfully wrongly

wronged

wrote *[text] — rote *[learn]

wrung *[squeezed] — rung *[ladder, bell]

wry *[humour] — rye *[grain]

wryly

wu — woo

wud — wood *[trees]
would *[would go]

wuff — woof

wulf — wolf

wull	wool
wully	woolly
wuman	woman
wume	womb
wunder	wonder *[think]*
wurd	word
wuren't	weren't [were not]
wurk	work
wurl	whirl
wurld	world
wurldwide	worldwide
wurr	were *[we were late]*
	whirr *[sound]*
wuz	was
wyde	wide
wyfe	wife
wyle	while *[when]*
	wile *[trick]*

X-ray X-rays

[x-raying x-rayed]

xma eczema

Xmas

xylophone

yacht yachting
yachtsman yachtswoman
yak
yam
yank [yanking yanked]
yap [yapping yapped]
yard
yashmak
yaun — yawn
yawn [yawning yawned]
yeah
year yearly
yeast
yeer — year
yeest — yeast
yeh — yeah
yeild — yield
yeld — yelled
yell [yelling yelled]
yellow yellower yellowest
yellowish
yelo — yellow
yelp [yelping yelped]
yen
yer — year
yere — year
yes
yesterday

yet
yeti
yew *[tree]* — ewe *[sheep]*
you *[person]*
yews *[trees]* — use *[apply]*
yield [yielding yielded]
yippee
yoak — yoke *[round neck]*
yolk *[egg]*
yodel [yodelling yodelled]
yoga
yogert — yoghurt
yoghurt
yolk *[egg]* — yoke *[neck]*
yoow — you
yorn — yawn
yors — yours
yorself — yourself
yot — yacht
you *[person]* — yew *[tree]*
ewe *[sheep]*
you'd *[you had, would]*
youf — youth
you'll *[you will]* — Yule *[Xmas]*
young youngster
youniform — uniform
your *[owns]* — you're *[you are]*

yours faithfully
yours sincerely
yourself yourselves

yous	use
you'sd	used

youth youthful
youth hostel
you've *[you have]
yo-yo

yu	yew *[tree]*
	you *[person]*
yud	you'd *[you had, would]*

Yule *[Xmas]* you'll *[you will]*
yummy yum-yum

yung	young
yunger	younger
yuse	use
yuth	youth

zap [zapping zapped]
zapper
zeal zealous
zebra zebra-crossing
zeel zeal
zero zeros
zest
zigzag
[zigzagging zigzagged]
zilophone xylophone
Zimmer™-frame
zinc
zip [zipping zipped]
ziro zero
zoan zone
zodiac
zombie
zone [zoning zoned]
zonked
zoo zoo-keeper
Zoolu Zulu
zoom [zooming zoomed]
zoom lens
zu zoo
Zulu
zylofone xylophone